A BC OF HERALDRY

ABC OF HERALDRY

BY

GUY CADOGAN ROTHERY

AUTHOR OF
"SYMBOLS, EMBLEMS, AND DEVICES," "ARMORIAL
INSIGNIA OF THE PRINCES OF WALES, WITH A
DISCUSSION OF THE SYMBOLIC MEANING OF
FEATHERS, AND OF BIRDS AND DRAGONS"
ETC. ETC.

*With 13 Illustrations in colour
and 314 in half-tone and line*

LONDON
STANLEY PAUL & CO
31 ESSEX STREET, STRAND, W.C.

" In a symbol there is concealment and yet
revelation . . . there is ever, more or less
distinctly and directly, some embodiment
and revelation of the Infinite ; the Infinite
is made to blend itself with the Finite, to
stand, visible, and as it were, attainable
there."—THOMAS CARLYLE, " Sartor Re-
sartus."

First published in 1915

I. BADGE "OF PEACE" OF
THE BLACK PRINCE.

II. COUNTY OF CORNWALL.

III. COUNTY OF CHESTER.

IV. DUCHY OF CORNWALL.

V. SIR ROGER DE CLARENDON
(NATURAL SON OF THE
BLACK PRINCE).

VI. SAXONY.

TYPES OF EARLY ARMORY.

[Frontispiece.

PREFACE

HERALDRY possesses so many points of interest—artistic, historical and social—that it has been thought well to add this volume to the series. While my preoccupations have been mainly artistic and historical, I have endeavoured to give the necessary practical information.

Both the artist and the collector are advised to study the subject not merely in books and manuscripts, but in the rich examples of contemporary work seen in our cathedrals, churches and domestic buildings. The Victoria and Albert Museum, South Kensington, affords a splendid review of heraldic decoration, in different periods and countries.

In compiling this volume I have made use of some chapters contributed to various technical and other periodicals.

Illustrations have been largely selected with the desire to show the diversity of treatment in time and place.

I have to thank Mr. John J. Pegge for the instructive series of achievements belonging to the Craft Guilds of Durham. It is necessary to give a word of warning about these. Mr. Pegge says: "The Guild coats of arms (the hand-painted examples are hung in the Durham Guildhall) of the several companies appear to be those of London, York and other ancient towns, but the grouping of the various trades forming a guild is peculiar." On examination it will be found that the Durham blazoning does not always tally with that of London or Edinburgh, that in some cases the trades assume different names, and that the grouping of two crafts is not always represented on the shield.

The photograph of the quaint coat of the Royal Tudor Arms from Clifton was kindly sent by Dr. A. B. Prowse, of that town. I am indebted to Mr. Augustus Steward for the three fine book-plates by his talented pupil, Mr. G. Friend.

G. C. R.

CONTENTS

CONTENTS

LIST OF ILLUSTRATIONS

b

INTRODUCTION

ALTHOUGH the origin of heraldry cannot be traced with certainty, yet it is clear that the adoption of tribal, national and personal badges began in prehistoric times ; at all events we find traces of such a custom even in the rude remains of forgotten races. Hence some writers trace the beginning of heraldry very far back indeed. No doubt this may be justified if we look for the germs of the art, which certainly adds enormously to the interest of our study. In Greek sculpture, in the paintings and incised designs traced on ancient pottery, we find a number of well-defined symbols constantly associated with mythical or historical heroes, as well as with races of people. Often these symbols are borne on shields, adorn helmets or standards, just in the style so common in our own middle ages, in China and Japan, and, indeed, even among semi-barbarian and savage tribes. All the gods had their special attributive symbols, and these were so far hereditary that they were adopted by their demi-god terrestrial "sons" and "daughters." Much the same condition of things prevailed in connection with Roman and Etruscan social conditions. This adoption of symbols was also carried very far by the Assyrians, Hittites and other Asiatic peoples. In Egypt, not only were there symbols for individual rulers, but family badges common to the several dynasties, and the kingly and priestly sons of the great gods also bore the divine symbols. Moreover, each territorial division had its elaborate symbol, usually combining naturalistic plant and animal forms with purely conventional designs, while the lotus stood as the peculiar attribute of Northern Egypt, and the papyrus of the Southern

xvii

regions, the union of the two parts of the fertilising Nile being represented by the intertwining of the stems of these plants in intricate knots. Symbolism, being co-eval with the first glimmerings of human intelligence, is a thing of natural evolution, erratic in its modes of growth, and in its essentials independent of time or clime. However, the heralds, having made symbols their chief props, it is necessary to attempt more or less systematic tracings of the Protean manifestations peculiar to particular emblems. This aspect of the subject will be dealt with more fittingly when the different heraldic charges are under discussion.

SHIELD FROM GREEK
VASE.

For our immediate purpose, it must be remembered that heraldry strictly so-called only became a science when laws were laid down for its guidance, and when the various symbols adopted were recognised as hereditary. It seems certain that this did not come about until the eleventh century, when nobles fought in armour, and each led his particular body of retainers into the field. In this quite restricted sense, the Emperor Frederick Barbarossa is believed to be the real father of the art. Even long after his day nobles were allowed to do much as they listed in the matter of adopting and varying coat armour. In England, although two heralds, Norroy and Surroy, were appointed by Edward I and Clarencieux by Henry IV in 1411, it was not until the reign of Henry V that proclamation was made forbidding any one to assume armorial bearings without permission from the King or his heralds. It was the Earl Marshal's Court which upheld this law, though the King himself was the final authority. However, it was not until some centuries later that Heralds' Visitations to enforce its rulings were instituted. During these visitations the heralds went round from town to town, summoning all knights, esquires and gentlemen to appear and register their arms, all marriages, births, deaths, and other family events. These visitations took place at irregular intervals, eaeh circuit lasting for about eighteen months to two years. The records of these journeys are mines of information, though perhaps not so interesting as the older Rolls of Arms, giving metrical or prose descriptions of bearings of knights at various periods. The paintings on some of these Rolls demonstrate the great flexibility of practice in those days, together with the growing tendency to crystallise vague guiding principles into exact rules.

Henry V was a great patron of heraldry ; he instituted the office of Garter King of Arms, and as his pursuivant, Blue Mantle. It was also during his reign that coat armour became regularly hereditary, and descended from father to son, the eldest alone wearing the shield as his father did before him ; the younger ones having to make some difference, such as adding a border, or using other marks of cadency. The oldest coats-of-arms are generally very plain, and have few charges besides the Ordinaries. With time, owing to this practice of the younger branches of a family accumulating charges, altering the outlines of others, changing their colour, and assuming ornamented borders, while simple knights often accepted the privilege of placing on their shields some charge from the armorials of their overlords, the great feudal chiefs, heraldry became more complicated.

Sir James Lawrence, speaking of heraldry and nobility, in his " Nobility of the British Gentry," thus explains the original use of, and the different methods of obtaining, armorial bearings : " Any individual who distinguished himself may be said to ennoble himself. A prince judging an individual worthy of notice gave him patent letters of nobility. In these letters were emblazoned the arms that were to distinguish his shield. By this shield he was to be known, or *nobilis*. A plebeian had no blazonry on his shield, because he was *ignobilis*, or unworthy of notice. Hence arms are the criterion of nobility. Whoever has a shield of arms is a nobleman. In every country in Europe, without exception, a grant of arms, or letters patent of nobility, is conferred on all the descendants." Thus it will be seen that the essential part of heraldry to chivalry was the hereditary character of coat armour. It may be as well to explain that this appellation of a coat-of-arms originated from the practice of embroidering the family insignia on the surcoat, a garment worn over the armour or shirt of mail. These surcoats in later times were used only by heralds, by whom they are

SEAL AND COUNTER SEAL, GEOFFROI DE CHATEAUBRIAND, BRITTANY, 1217.

still worn, when on official duties, and by pages and menials of princely or noble houses. But arms were not only seen on the surcoat. They appeared on the caparisons of a knight's horse, on his shield and other accoutrements, were embroidered on the wall hangings of the castle hall, and lent greater authority to his engraved seal.

From the arms of the head of the State to arms of concession, there are altogether ten degrees : First, arms of dominion, or national armorial bearings borne by sovereigns. Secondly, we have arms of pretension, or armorial bearings adopted by sovereigns of kingdoms or provinces over which they are actually reigning. (If a man marries an heiress, he is entitled to wear her arms in an escutcheon of pretence placed over his own, but this properly belongs to the eighth degree.) Thirdly, arms of community, such as the arms of bishops' sees, of towns, universities, colleges and corporate bodies.

Fourthly, arms of patronage, which are arms of community worn by the occupants of various offices of responsibility and dignity. Fifthly, arms of succession ; arms borne by the inheritors of fiefs, manors, either by will or donation. Sixthly, arms of assumption, when a victor adopts the whole or part of the insignia of the vanquished. A sub-division of arms of assumption, also known as arms of pretension, are those borne by a non-ruling claimant to territorial dignities. Seventhly, paternal arms ; the arms descending from father to son. Eighthly, arms of alliance ; arms borne in a shield of pretence by the husband of an heiress and then quartered by the descendants in order to show their descent. Ninthly, arms of adoption, borne by strangers in blood in accordance with the wishes laid down by will or other legal mode of donation, or arms borne by an adopted child of the original bearer ; but before adoption express permission must be obtained from the sovereign. And, tenthly, arms of concession ; armorial bearings ; parts of armorial bearings ; or special charges given by a sovereign to a subject. These last arms or charges are also commonly known as augmentations.

During the Heralds' Visitations two chief claims to the right to bear arms were recognised : (1) the claim to ownership of certain bearings by repute, (2) the right to bear by a direct grant. Evidence as to ownership by repute was either aural, as most of it was in the celebrated case of Sir Richard le Scrope against Sir Robert Grosvenor before the High Court of Chivalry, which was commenced in August 1385, with revised judgment delivered by King Richard II in 1390 ; or according to evidence afforded by seals, banners or monuments ; or that afforded by the Rolls. These last are a series of most interesting documents, in the form of long rolls of parchment, giving blazonings of arms borne by different individuals at certain events (such as the metrical description in Norman-French of the siege of Carlaverock, a Scottish border stronghold taken by Edward I in 1300, with an account of the arms of the great nobles and knights present). There are many of these Rolls, but none older than a little before the middle of the thirteenth century.

Grants of arms were made by the King or his deputy, the Earl Marshal, or his deputies, the Heralds, and were recorded on formal parchment documents. It is probable that up to the reign of Richard II the great territorial lords still preserved their feudal privilege of bestowing armorial bearings on their vassals and friends. In modern practice all arms are, or should be, borne by grace of a Grant or a Confirmation, issued by the College of Arms in England, the Lyon Office in Scotland, or Ulster King of Arms in Ireland, with the direct sanction of the Crown. Unless there is direct and clear evidence of a coat-of-arms having descended from father to son since a grant was made, or an entry recorded in one of the Visitations, persons before using arms are supposed to present a properly authenticated pedigree to the heralds, and then obtain a confirmation to their right to wear the coat-of-arms they claim. Persons receiving certain high honours, or offices of honour, from the Crown, must have arms, and then, if they and their immediate ascendants, have not borne arms, a search, involving genealogical work, is made to connect the person with some recorded coat. If no clear connection can be established, then a grant is made. But anybody who desires can make an application for a grant of arms, and if certain conditions are fulfilled a grant will be issued. In making these new grants, it has been too often the habit to bestow on an applicant, if not the identical coat of an old family of the same name, then some " colourable imitation thereof," even though the applicant cannot prove alliance. All new grants ought to be thoroughly distinctive to avoid misconceptions. This point will be clearly understood on referring to Chapter XIII on " Differences and Marks of Cadency," where the early principles of recording heraldically blood and feudal relationships are shown.

There are three principal divisions of coat armour—the field (or ground), the tinctures (metals, colours, and furs) and the charges or symbols.

The field is the ground of the shield or banner, and for the better description or blazoning of armorial bearings the shield has been divided into several parts.

It must first be explained that in describing armorial bearings, it is always assumed that they are on a shield or surcoat borne by the owner, and the description is from the wearer's point of view. Thus what the ordinary spectator regards as the left side of a shield is known to the herald as the dexter side, while the right becomes the heraldic sinister. This must always be kept in mind when blazoning is in question. We may now pass on to the divisions of the shield. These are : (B) Middle Chief, or middle of the upper part ; (A) Dexter Chief (left upper part) ; (C) Sinister Chief (right upper part) ; (E) Fess Point, or middle of the shield ; (D) Honour Point, between the Fess Point and the Middle Chief ; (H) Middle Base, or lower point of field ; (G) Dexter Base (left lower part) ; (I) Sinister Base (right lower part). With the complications introduced into feudal heraldry during the fifteenth century and

POINTS OF THE SHIELD.

onwards, such minutæ as these became very necessary in order to avoid confusion, but they also tended to overlay the science with many fanciful notions as to the most honoured parts of a field, notions which most assuredly did not exist to worry knights in the days when heraldry was most simple, beautiful and important.

The surface of the shield may be divided by a horizontal, perpendicular, or diagonal line ; or by a combination of these lines. A field thus divided is said to be " per " or " party per," with the descriptive epithet following. A field divided by a horizontal line is said to be " per fess " ; by a vertical line, " per pale " ; by a diagonal line, " per bend " or " per bend sinister," as the case may be ; by an upright line and a horizontal line, " per cross " or " quarterly " ; by the right and left diagonal lines, " per saltire " ; if the lower parts of the right and left bends are brought to the honour point, the shield is divided " per chevron," which the French heralds term "mantelé." A field divided in three parts by two horizontal lines is " tierced per fess " ; if the lines are perpendicular the field is " tierced per pale." A field may be (though this is rare in practice) divided per fess and bend, or per pale and bend. A field divided per fess, per pale, per bends dexter and sinister is said to be " gyrony." A field may be borne " paly," divided by a number of perpendicular lines ; " barry," divided by a number of horizontal lines ; " lozengy " or " fusily," divided by a number of lines from left to right crossing others from right to left ; " paly-bendy," perpendicular lines crossed by diagonal lines ; or " barry-bendy," if

LINES OF DIVISION : RAYONNY ; URDY ; DOVETAILED ; DANCETE ;
INDENTED ; POTENTÉ ; NEBULÉ ; WAVY.

divided by horizontal and diagonal lines ; if divided by horizontal lines crossed by perpendicular lines it is said to be " chequy " or " checky "; if by a series of wedges, it is " pily," or, as some rather unnecessarily term it, " pily counter-pily." It should be noted that if the space between two horizontal lines (forming a fess) is divided into squares, alternately of metal and colour, it is said to be compony or gobony ; if there are two such rows, it is said to be counter-compony ; if three or more, then it is chequy. All these terms will be better understood after a perusal of the next two chapters.

The divisional lines described above may be either straight or variously shaped ; such as an " embattled " line, also em-

battled grady, a " potenté " line (like the Greek key pattern),
" wavy " (or " undée "), " indented," " invected," " nebulé,"
(or cloud-like), " urdy," " danceté," " embattled," " raguly "
(which is a line with the
battlements at a slant),
"dove-tailed," " en-
grailed " or " bevilled."
Such lines of demarcation
are also used in drawing
certain classes of charges.

LINES OF DIVISION : EMBATTLED ;
ENGRAILED ; INVECTED.

The tinctures comprise
two metals, nine colours
(five of which are in
general use), and three furs, with their variations. The terms
employed to describe them in formal heraldic language are
old French. Some heralds (of the seventeenth century),
in order to give additional importance to the science, as
they thought, invented the plan of emblazoning the arms
of peers and peeresses with the names of precious stones,
and those of sovereigns and princes with the names of planets
and other heavenly bodies instead of using the ordinary terms
for tinctures. In drawings or engravings these colours are
represented by dots and differently arranged lines, an invention ascribed by some to Colombière, and by other authorities
to Silvestro di Pietrasancta, who both flourished during the
seventeenth century. When the colours are not represented
by lines, numerals or symbols are adopted instead.

TINCTURES

1. Gold . Or, represented by dots. . . .
   Topaz.
   Sol, represented by o.

2. Silver . Argent, represented by a plain surface.
   Crystal.
   Luna, represented by ☽ .

3. Red . Gules, represented by perpendicular lines.
   Ruby.
   Mars, represented by ♂ .

ERMINE.

ERMINES.

PEAN.

ERMINE.

VAIR.

POTENT COUNTER
POTENT.

VAIR.

COUNTER VAIR.

POTENT.

COUNTER POTENT.

FURS.

xxvi

4. Blue . Azure, represented by horizontal lines.
Sapphire.
Jupiter, represented by ♃.

5. Black . Sable, represented by perpendicular and horizontal lines crossing each other.
Diamond.
Saturn, represented by ♄.

6. Green . Vert or sinople, represented by lines from dexter chief to sinister base.
Emerald.
Venus, represented by ♀.

7. Purple . Purpure, represented by lines from sinister chief to dexter base.
Amethyst.
Mercury, represented by ☿.

There are four additional colours sometimes mentioned by heralds, which, however, are seldom used except for special charges, external accessories and for liveries. These colours are " sanguine " or "murrey "—a deep blood-red (sardonyx, Dragon's Tail), represented by lines from dexter chief to sinister base ; and " tenné " or " orange " (hyacinth, Dragon's Head), represented by lines from sinister to dexter base, crossed by horizontal lines ; and flesh colour, sometimes called " carnation." Bleue celeste, a light sky blue ; an ashen grey and brown are also, though rarely, seen.

The furs are " ermine," white with black spots, and its four modifications—" ermines," black with silver spots ; " erminetes," black with white spots ; " erminois," black with gold spots ; and " pean," gold with black spots. The ermine spot varies a good deal, but the most usual form is like an inverted clove, with three sepals showing, and three dots, one and two, above. " Vair " is represented by blue and white shields, or glasses, in horizontal rows, the bases of the white resting on the base of the blue. This fur has also one modification, which is termed " counter-vair," in which the glasses of one colour are placed base to base. " Vair " is always emblazoned argent and azure, and counter vair, or and azure. If other tinctures are used, they must be specified. " Potent " is represented by crutch-shaped charges; it is emblazoned argent and azure, the base of one colour being placed on the base of one of metal; and its modifications " counter-potent," sometimes termed " vairy-cuppy," which is of the same tinctures as " potent," but the crutch-shaped charges of one colour have their bases placed against the bases of one of the same colour; and " potent, counter-potent " in which the arrangement is different. Here again, if other colours are used, the tinctures must be specially named.

In describing a shield, the tincture of the field should be first mentioned. A shield may be parti-coloured, as we have seen when describing the divisions. For instance, a shield divided down the middle by a perpendicular line, the left side green (vert), and the right red (gules), would be described thus : Party per pale gules and vert. It is a strict general rule that metal must not be placed on metal, or colour on colour.

That is to say, if the field is of gold or silver, the charges thereon must be of colour or fur. However, many exceptions are allowed. Thus a parti-tinctured shield, where both metal and colour are used, or a fur-covered field, may bear charges of either metal or colour. On the other hand, if the parti field is half metal and half colour, it is usual to " counter-change "

ST. BARTHOLOMEW'S HOSPITAL, LONDON.

the charges. Thus the arms of St. Bartholomew's Hospital are : per pale argent and sable a fess counter-changed, which are the arms also assigned to Geoffrey Chaucer, the father of English poetry, with the tinctures altered to argent and gules. Rodenstein, a German feudal leader of the early fourteenth century, bore : per pale or and gules, a fess counterchanged. Then again, the accessories of a charge are not subject to such a rule. For instance, a silver or gold lion, or other animal, may have tongue and claws of red or blue, if the field be blue or red, while if the field is gold or silver, the coloured beast may have tongue and claws of silver or gold. Crowns, coronets, chains attached to animals are also free from the general law. So are marks of cadency. Occasionally arms violating this rule are found. These are what Continental heralds call " armes à enquirire," arms to be inquired about, as being exceptional. Such are the arms of the Kingdom of Jerusalem, first bestowed on Geoffrey de Bouillon : argent, a cross potent between four crosses, all or.[1]

While discussing this point something may be said of diapering, though this will be described more at length at a later stage. Diapering is a method of decorating plain sur-faces by tracing thereon a faint design of a running floral or geometrical pattern. These patterns are often quite com-plicated, but they must be subordinate to the general design, as they are non-essential and merely ornamental. They are of importance just here, because often enough this diapering of thin outline running patterns may be carried out in silver upon gold, or gold upon silver, even red on blue, or blue on red, and so on. As a matter of fact this is not an infraction of the general rule, because the diaper had no heraldic value, and being non-essential is regarded as non-existent except from the purely decorative point of view.

Gold may be represented by yellow, and silver by white, but even when this is so, they are regarded as metals.

The sixteenth and seventeenth century heralds appear to have paid some attention to the symbolical attributes of colour in designing arms, and no doubt this was to a certain extent a ruling motive of the eleventh to thirteenth century man in selecting so largely the royal gold, the martial red, and the celestial blue.

---

[1] Some writers state that the five crosses represented the wounds of Christ, and that they were originally emblazoned gules, which gave a better colour symbolism. The crosses were subsequently changed to gold so as to make the bearings a striking contrast to any other royal or feudal shield.

I. WALES.

II. NORTH WALES.

III. POWYS.

IV. ELYSTAN GLORUDD.

V. OWEN GLENDOWER.

VI. CARNARVON.

WELSH PRINCELY ARMS.

[1

ABC OF HERALDRY

CHAPTER I

THE ORDINARIES

A CERTAIN class of what may justly be called the fundamentals of heraldic ornament appear to be little else than structural parts of the shield, slightly developed for decorative and distinctive purposes.

These include at least eight of those bands—horizontal, perpendicular, diagonal and their combinations—which have been called the Ordinaries, or the Honourable Ordinaries, and are generally held, by the most competent of the old heraldic authorities, to be ten in number.

It is quite true that even in remote times some of these had assumed a distinctly symbolic form, as we shall see, but their origin seems unquestionably to belong to the reign of structural members, developed and embellished. Now, at the dawn of heraldic science, as these ordinaries already existed on the escutcheons of the principal nobles, and indeed on nearly all of the earlier coats-of-arms, the heralds, who were appointed for the purpose of introducing a little order and method in the science, classed them as the first and highest order of heraldic charges. It is hardly astonishing to find that nearly every one of these ten different charges has a special meaning or legend attached to it.

One of the greatest contrasts between the earlier and probably the best period of the art—say from the eleventh

I

century to the thirteenth century—and the growing alliance between ill-regulated invention and extravagant formalism which began with the sixteenth and lasted to the middle of the nineteenth century, is the simplicity of the primitive specimens, compared with the overcrowded, out-of-balance compositions of the decadence. Naturally enough, the enlightened attach a particular value to the escutcheon according to its simplicity, as the escutcheon of the younger branches of a family often had new additions to distinguish them from the elder.

ROCHESTER

In later times, however, with us, as also on the Continent, the escutcheon was valued by the number of charges, in many cases the ordinaries as well as the field being heavily charged. In English heraldry it was always allowable to emblazon the honourable ordinaries with almost any common or minor charge, but the practice is not so much resorted to as on the Continent. Throgmorton bears : gules, on a chevron argent, three bars gemells sable ; and Trenowith, Cornwall, argent, on a fess sable, three chevronels couched sinister silver. The Count of Neuburg bore : or, on a pale gules three chevrons argent. Many of the ordinaries are borne " over all," that is to say, they are placed across the charged field. If the charge happens to be an animal, it is said to be " debruised." If one ordinary is borne across another, then the term " surmounted " is used.

The principal ordinary is the " chief " ; it occupies the upper part of the shield and should fill a third of the surface of the field. In many old writers this upper part of the shield is alluded to as the " Sovereign."

Each ordinary has a certain number of diminutives, or

modifications of the parent charge. In the case of the " chief," its diminutive is the " fillet," one-fourth of the chief, and is always placed in the lower portion of the " chief." A chief may be borne on a field with any other ordinary except the fess or its diminutive, the bar. In practice it is usual to allow rather less than a third of the field for the chief, to distinguish the bearing more readily from a field divided per fess, which cuts the shield horizontally in two. Most of the other ordinaries, though supposedly occupying a third of the field, are slightly under their allowance.

The " pale," second in importance, is a band, occupying one-third of the shield, from top to bottom. Its diminutives are the " palet," half the size of the pale, and the " endorse," which is half the size of the palet.[1] The word endorse comes from the French *endorse*, to place back to back. A pale when emblazoned between two endorses is said to be " endorsed " or " indorsed." A pale between its two endorses is sometimes said to be " cotised," but erroneously, as will be seen on perusal of the following paragraph. A curious variation of the pale is seen in the arms of d'Aussez, Normandy : argent, on a chief azure three martlets of the first, a saw blade in pale, the teeth to the sinister. That is to say, a pale with the sinister side invected. From France also we have a modification of the palet, De Briez bearing : or three palets couped and fitchy at foot gules. This gives us three stakes.

The " bend " represents a band, one-third of the shield, crossing from the dexter chief to the sinister base. The bend has three diminutives ; they are the " bendlet " (sometimes called a " garter "), the " cotice," and the " ribbon." A shield divided into several parts by lines " in bend " is said to be " coticed." When a bend is charged with symbols, these take the diagonal trend of the ordinary—they are placed on the slant.

---

[1] In every case the first diminutive ought to be one-half of its parent charge ; the second one-half of the first ; the third one-half of the second. This rule does not apply to the chief, the saltire, or the quarter.

The " bend sinister " is the bend, or bend dexter, reversed, coming from the sinister chief to the dexter base. The " scarpe " and the " baton " are its diminutives. The baton, variously called " baston " and " batoon," is the charge used by heralds as a mark of bastardy.[1] It is sometimes borne " couped," when its extremities do not touch the sides of the shield. This was a special privilege, and at one time

rarely conceded, except to the illegitimate offspring of royalty. Another mode of lessening the disgrace of this charge was to have it reversed, a privilege conferred only in extraordinary cases, After the bravery displayed on the battlefield against the English by John the Bastard of Orleans, Charles VII allowed him to turn his baton from sinister to dexter. A like boon was granted to the Earl of Murray by his sister,

BEND.

Mary Queen of Scots. More on this subject will be found in the chapter on " Differences and Marks of Cadency." Gelre gives the arms of Raman von Konigstein as : per bend or and sable, the upper half of a bend sinister argent.

The " fess " is a horizontal band in the middle of the shield, and occupies one-third of its surface. It was supposed to represent the waistband, one of the symbols of knighthood or high military command. The officers' and non-commissioned officers' scarves, still worn in our army, are relics of this ancient scarf of authority. But as a matter of fact the fess is one of the constructural members of the shield. The " bar," the " closet," and the " barrulet," this last always borne in couples, are the diminutives of this charge.

The " chevron " is formed by two bands rising from the sides of the shield and meeting in a point in the centre. It is one of the charges formerly given to younger members of families, and is highly prized. In English heraldry the lower

---

[1] The term " bastard bar " has been popularly, but erroneously, given to this symbol ; the bar is a diminutive of the " fess," and therefore the term " bar " cannot be applied to the diminutive of the " bend sinister."

EXAMPLES OF THE CHEVRON.

WEAVERS' GUILD (DURHAM GUILDS).

I. BLACKSMITHS.   II. LORIMERS.   III. LOCKSMITHS.
IV. CUTLERS.   V. BLADESMITHS.

lines of the chevron commence just above its dexter and sinister base, and the apex ends about the honour point. In Continental practice, this ordinary commences from a lower point and rises higher, so becoming more acute. Roughly it may be said to be composed of the lower halves of the bend and the bend sinister conjoined in chief. A chevron is sometimes borne " rompu en pointe," that is broken at the apex ; or " coupé," cut off from the sides of the shield. The diminutives are the " chevronel " and the " couple-close," which last is always borne in couples, and often one on each side of the chevron, when the chevron is said to be " couple-closed." When the field is covered with couple-closes it is said to be chevronée. Sometimes a chevron

CHEVRON, WITH SINISTER CANTON.

CHEVRON, PATÉE AT POINT.

is borne reversed, as in the arms of the town of Newport : azure a chevron reversed, or. A chevron and a chevron reversed, interlaced, form a curious kind of saltire, probably due to the amalgamation of two coats. It is seen in the shield of Lagrenée : gules, a chevron or interlaced with a chevron reversed argent. Many heralds hold that the chevron represents the principal rafters of a gable roof, to which the term is still applied in the French language, and hence it is an appropriate charge for the founders of a family ; another theory is that it symbolically represents a park gate. Really it belongs to the class of structural strengthenings, and symbolically it appears to form a section of the extremely ancient and widespread wavy line (found in Rome and Greece, in Asia, Africa and America) representing water. Indeed, it is notable that the pale, the fess, the bend and the chevron, either argent, azure or sable, often appear on the shields of towns noted for their rivers, or on those of men who have won fame by their connection with rivers or the sea.

The following bearings of the chevron and its diminutives are of special interest. Among the feudal coats we find : Berkeley : gules, a chevron argent ; Clare : or, three chevronels gules ; Fitzwalter : or, a fess between two chevrons gules. Tourney bore : or, a chevron couched dexter gules ; whilst Bightine bore : purpure, a chevron couched sinister, or ; Holbeame : argent, a chevron inarched sable ; that is, supported by an arch. Robert Fitz-Hugh, Bishop of London, 1431–1436, bore : argent, three chevronels braced (or interlaced) in base or ; a chief of gold ; De la Rochefoucauld : barry argent and azure, over all three chevronels or, the top one couped at the summit. Von Viseleben had their shield chevronée reversed argent and gules.

The " cross " is a combination of the pale and the fess ; it is a favourite and much-valued charge. The ornamentation of heraldic crosses is so extraordinarily varied that this " honourable ordinary " is deserving of, and considered in, a chapter by itself.

The " saltire " is formed by bend dexter and bend sinister conjoined, and is also dealt with at length in the chapter on " Crosses."

ARGENT, A CHEVRON SURMOUNTED BY A PILE, BOTH SABLE, PIERCED OF THE FIELD.

The " pile " is in the form of a wedge, the point downwards. Its proper size is one-third of the shield in its upper part, but if it is charged its broadest end fills up two-thirds of the shield. A pile may be borne " transposed," that is to say, with the point uppermost. It may also come at a slant from the dexter or sinister chief, or dexter or sinister base. Sometimes two, or three, piles may be borne ; then their points do not reach the base of the shield. If there are three piles, they are now usually blazoned as " in point," that is to say, there is a thin wedge from the centre chief, and other wedges slanting from the dexter and sinister chiefs, their points almost meeting. A very broad pile used, especially in Continental practice, to take a coat-of-arms in marshalling, is called by the French a " chausse," and if reversed a " chape," while a reduced chape is a " cha-peronne." Shields so divided are said to be " chaussé," " chapé " and " chaperonné."

The tenth and last Honourable Ordinary is the " quarter," which occupies the upper dexter portion of the shield, con-sisting of one-fourth of its surface. It has one diminutive, the " canton," occupying one-eighth of the shield.

All the above charges may be " voided," a term applied to a charge when it has its centre removed, showing the field through it. The " voiding " may be of any shape ; a cross is voided " per cross," " per pale," or " per fess " ; but in such a case the shape of the voiding must be specially men-tioned, otherwise it would mean that the charge was " voided " of its own shape. Mr. Mark A. Lower, the author of " Curi-osities of Heraldry," says that this custom of voiding was adopted because the bearers had lost their patrimonies, and retained only the " shadow " of their ancient greatness. But there appears to be no evidence of this. As a rule voiding is either the result of charging one ordinary with another of its kind, either for the purpose of differencing, or for recording alliances ; or the adoption of an embroidered ornament. We constantly find modifications of this kind being introduced by painters or sculptors more intent in securing effective results than observing technical rules.

The terms " in pale," " in bend," etc., when applied to common charges, denote that they are borne disposed in the form of the ordinary mentioned. We have already seen that a shield is said to be " paly," " bendy," etc., when it is divided by several lines in the form of the ordinary mentioned, the number of divisions being also specified with the tinctures ; the first division being of the first-named, the second of the second, and so on alternately. As also already men-tioned a shield may be divided " per pale," " per bend," etc., when it is of two different tinctures and divided in the shape of the ordinary. The term " tierced " is applied to a shield which is divided into three parts ; it may be either " tierced in fess," " in pale," " in bend," " in bend sinister," or " in pall " (also called " en pairle "), according to the form of

THREE SHOVELS EN PAIRLE.

BOULOGNE-SUR-SEINE : PARTY
PER BEND SINISTER.

the three parts. German and French partition lines are occasionally extraordinarily complicated, forming odd geometrical patterns. For instance, we may have " party per pale potenté and per bend engrailed."

When any ordinary is pierced by a square hole it is said to be " square-pierced " ; but if, in the case of a cross, the whole of the intersecting portion is removed it is termed a cross " quarterly-pierced." Ordinaries may be simply " pierced," i.e., pierced with a round hole, and also " lozenge-pierced." As with the chevron all ordinaries are often borne " couped," that is to say, they have their extremities cut off, and so do not touch the sides of the

MANCHESTER : BENDLETS
ENHANCED.

shield ; some of them may also be " broken," or " rompu," when the ends instead of being cut off with a smooth edge are torn off and present a ragged edge. A fess, a pale and a bend may be borne " engoulé," that is to say, ending in the mouth of man or beast, placed at the edge of the shield, but within the field. Three of these charges, a fess, a bend and a chevron, together with their diminutive, may be borne " enhanced," that is, higher than the fess point, their proper place. This is the case with the three golden bendlets of Manchester, borne enhanced on a red field. They may also be borne " debased," that is lower than their proper position. On the feudal coat of Fitzwalter, described above, the chevron is borne both enhanced and debased.

CHAPTER II

THE SUB-ORDINARIES

THE Sub-Ordinaries, charges of lesser degree and supposedly of less antiquity than the honourable ordinaries,
are sometimes stated to be twelve in number and sometimes
more, the principal authorities disagreeing as to how many
and what charges should be included under this denomina-
tion. Many of these—the fret and the border, for instance—
partake, like the ordinaries, of a structural character—
strengthenings of the shield ; but others are more markedly
distinctive or symbolical in origin.

The " gyron " (from *gyrus*, a circle) is a term applied
to a shield when it is quartered and divided per cross and per
saltire, each division being alternately of metal and of colour.
An ordinary gyron is called " gyron of eight," but it may be
a gyron of only six, or of ten or twelve. Somewhat akin to

GYRON.

GYRON OF SIX.

this is that very curious device known as a " whirlpool,"
" gurge " or " gorge," a blue spiral ribbon, starting from the
fess point and circling round until it covers the silver field.
Quite an old type was represented by a series of diminishing
rings, one within the other. A gurge is always argent and

azure, unless other tinctures are specially mentioned. Both the gyron and the gurge are met with among quite primitive symbols in most parts of the world, and generally seem to have reference to elemental phenomena, seasonal changes, movement, whirlpools.

The " fret " is a combination of the baton and the cotise, interlaced by a lozenge. If the shield is covered with lattice-work it is termed " fretty," or " fretty cloué " when instead

FRET WITH PELLETS AT EACH POINT.   FRET, FLORY AT EACH POINT.   FRET WITH FOUNTAINS IN CLAIR-VOIES.

of being interlaced the dexter lattice is placed over the sinister bars and nailed. Certain charges, such as swords and lances, may be borne in trellis. For instance, the ancient Provençal family of De Villeneuve bear : gules, six golden lances in trellis, semée of inescutcheons, or. The terms " treille " and " trellis " are also used. The interspaces are sometimes termed clair-voies.

FRET.   FRET COUPED.   CHEQUY GULES AND AR-GENT, AN INESCUTCHEON ARGENT.

The " inescutcheon " is a small shield borne as a charge. It is usually placed in the fess-point, but must not be confounded with a shield of pretence. Three or more inescutcheons may be borne. Both the Scottish Hays and the Norman de Villiers bear three inescutcheons of gules on a field of silver.

The "border" or "bordure" is a broad band encircling the shield ; it is borne both plain and charged, and has been made of great use in distinguishing cadency and in differencing arms, as will be shown in Chapter XIII. Some heralds have enumerated the border with the honourable ordinaries. Its diminutives are two. The "orle," which, unlike the "border," does not touch the edges of the shield, is also described as an "inescutcheon voided" or a "false inescutcheon." The idea thus expressed is that the orle is really an inescutcheon with the centre removed. In Continental

BORDER.   ORLE.   DOUBLE TRESSURE
                                FLORY COUNTER FLORY.

practice it is sometimes as though the charge consisted of two shields superimposed on a third. The second diminutive is the "tressure," which is a thin orle and is almost invariably borne "flory," that is to say, adorned by six fleurs-de-lis. In the "tressure flory" the fleur-de-lis all point outwards, but if three point outwards and three inwards, then the charge is called a "tressure-flory counter-flory." This last is sometimes borne double, one tressure within another, as in the instance of the Scottish arms : or, a lion rampant within a double tressure flory counter flory, gules. This form of the tressure in Scotland is most highly esteemed, it being a royal charge, and was only granted to private individuals by a royal warrant, and then only in cases where the recipient had performed some great deed for the good of his sovereign or country. It was also granted to the families directly descended from the female members of the royal family. The tressure flory, however, was a common mark of difference.

The "pall" or "pallium," an ecclesiastical vestment and ornament, is a combination of the upper part of the saltire, and the lower part of the pale. It appears in the arms of the sees of Canterbury, Armagh and Dublin, and formerly in those of York. A pall couped, with the ends pointed, is called a "shakefork." Charges may be borne "in pall." For instance Bismarck bears: azure, three oak leaves argent in pall, conjoined to a trefoil in fess point or.

PALL.

The "flanches" are the dexter and sinister portions of the shield, when they are cut off from the rest by curved lines; they are always borne in pairs, and the fact of their sometimes being charged has made some authorities class them as honourable ordinaries. The diminutive of the flanche is the "flasque," or "voider," also always borne in pairs. Many of the early Greek shields were pierced flanche-wise, that is to say, had curved pieces cut out of their sides.

FLANCHES.

The "lozenge" has four sides, the upper and lower points acute, and the side ones obtuse. Its diminutives are the

LOZENGE.

FUSIL.

LOZENGY.

"rustre," or lozenge with a round hole through the centre (when the hole is square it is termed "square-pierced");

the " fusil," which has its upper and lower angles much more acute than the lozenge, and is always borne erect ; and the " mascle," a lozenge showing only a narrow rim, through which the field is seen. The " mascle " probably was intended to represent a link of chain armour. A field may be borne lozengy, fusily or masculy, that is, covered with lozenges, fusils or mascles. The Duke of Teck bears : lozengy or and sable. The Duke of Suabia bore : argent a fess fusily (or three fusils in fess), gules.

Among some of the most ancient charges are the " roundels," small circular charges, which are sometimes classed as sub-ordinaries. Roundels are called "bezants " when of or ; tinc-tured argent, " plates " ; gules, " torteaux " ; azure, " hurts " ; sable, " ogress," or " gunstone," or " pellets " ; vert, " pom-mes," or " pomeis " ; purpure, " golpes " or " wounds " ; sanguine, " guzes " ; tenné, " oranges." The plate is some-times borne barry of seven argent and azure, when it is called a " fountain." These names are of comparatively recent origin, as formerly the heralds acknowledged bezants (from the golden Byzantines coins, familiar to the Crusading armies), plates (from the Spanish word for silver, *plata*), and torteaux,

CHINESE MONAD.

which were always men-tioned with their colour. These circular plates and small globes are among the earliest and most widespread symbols, representing the moon as a rule. When adorned with a whirl, or, as in that very ancient Eastern emblem, a circle enclos-ing two tadpole - like figures, they stand for the diurnal journey of the sun—night and day —the conflict between good and evil, the eternity of life. In China this is generally a venerated symbol, in which the figures are painted white and black, representing respectively the active or male principle, and the passive or female principle. This last symbol is greatly honoured in many Asiatic countries, and may be found in certain of the heraldic badges of Japanese feudal houses. The fountain also partakes of this early universal symbolism, standing for the fertilising water of the earth. In heraldry bezants and plates have been largely employed to symbolise both travel and commerce. On the other hand, they are often martial in character, as in the case of the three silver cannon-balls on the black fess, granted by Charles II to Admiral Sir William Penn, father of William Penn the Quaker settler of Pennsylvania, on the capture of Jamaica. All roundels may be charged. We have seen the plate with its three bars wavy of blue converted into a fountain. Another notable instance is the chief golden pill of the Florentine Medici adorned with the fleur-de-lis granted by Francis I.

An " annulet," or plain ring, really a separate charge, suggestive of the circle of eternity, but heraldically more directly connected with the tournament tilting-ring, has been described as a " false roundel," that is, a pierced or voided roundel.

The " mullet " and " star " have sometimes been classed among the sub-ordinaries. The mullet is a charge representing a spur-rowel, has five points and may be pierced. The star has six points or more ; they are always wavy, but, if it has more than six points, only every other one should be represented as wavy. The mullet and star were respectively military and ecclesiastical charges.

Billets are small long rectangular figures, variously supposed to represent parchment rolls, plates of metal or billets of wood. They may be of any colour, are sometimes (though rarely) charged, and are frequently borne powdered over the field, when the shield is said to be " billettée." They are frequently found on grants made to lawyers and learned clerks.

Flames of fire, when borne alone, may be counted as sub-ordinaries. They are borne as symbols of bravery and valour of the original bearer, ever impatient to lift his eyes and

thoughts upwards ; always thinking of and aspiring to perform, and no doubt sometimes having accomplished, brave
deeds. The charge is often seen on the Continent. Fire-
bombs, fire-buckets, fire-beacons, and torches in flames are
of more frequent occurrence, but these cannot be classed as
sub-ordinaries ; they belong to the vast number of common
charges.

EXAMPLES OF ORDINARIES AND SUB-ORDINARIES.

ARMS OF THE BUTCHERS, GOLDSMITHS, PLUMBERS, PEWTERERS, POTTERS, PAINTERS AND GLAZIERS (DURHAM GUILDS).

16]

CHAPTER III

THE CROSS AND ITS VARIATIONS

THIS device, which is one of the most highly esteemed of the Ordinaries, as well as a much varied charge, owes its place in heraldry as the accepted symbol of Christianity. But it is a very ancient religious symbol, being found in early Egyptian art, chiefly under the form of the cross patée (cross with expanded limbs), representing the four "gateways" or quarters of the world, and the tau or T cross, apparently a combination of the pillar (tree, emblem of fertility) and the lintel (the cover of heavens), the whole representing strength. This tau cross with the addition of an ovoid loop at the top, becomes the ankh, or symbol of life. In the ancient art of Asia the cross generally appears in the shape of the Swastika, or cross cramponée, with the extremities bent to right or left, representing at once the "gateways"—East, West, North and South—and the diurnal journey of the sun.

SWASTIKA OR CROSS CRAMPONÉE.

In Christian art the cross represents the Passion of Christ, and also His Church. In decorative design the principal forms are the Latin *crux immissa*, with a long lower limb; the Greek, with all four limbs of equal length; St. Andrew's, or cross in the form of a letter X (*crux decussata*); and the tau (*crux commissa*). The crucifix is the Latin cross bearing the effigy of the Savour nailed thereon. The Passion or Calvary cross is a Latin cross, bearing the crown of thorns, label, nails, and having the lance with reed and sponge placed at the back. A Latin cross elevated on three steps is said to be " graded," the steps representing Faith, Hope and Charity. Frequently the cross is represented as diffusing light, either in the form of a glory or rays from the point of intersection of the four limbs, or from the entire cross. In the crucifix the Head is frequently surrounded by a glory, while light radiates from the wounds.

In heraldry the cross is a combination of the pale and fess, the extremities touching the edge of the shield. It is of the Greek form, the four limbs being of equal width, and should occupy a fifth of the shield, or if charged one-third. The Latin cross is rarely used except as a badge or crest. These two are different forms of the ordinary. But there are very many variations of these, some of which may be classed as their diminutives, though most of the crosses mentioned below are generally treated as common charges. The following list has been made as complete as possible.

A cross flory is perhaps one of the most frequent charges ; it is ornamented at the extremities of its limbs by fleurs-de-lis ; it is a device of one of the French monarchs, who adorned plain crosses with the national emblems, and bestowed these honourable augmentations on favourites or great captains. Some writers give a cross fleury. It is a Greek cross couped

CROSS FLORY.   CROSS FLEURS-DE-LIS.   CROSS PATONCE.   CROSS BOTONY.

and ornamented, with fleur-de-lis, whilst in the cross flory the fleur-de-lis forms part of the cross. The cross patonce is very much like the cross flory, and undoubtedly owes its existence to an accidental alteration made by some careless painter of armorial bearings ; its terminations expand into three points, but do not display a distinct representation of the fleur-de-lis as the parent charge does. The cross botonée, botony, or by some styled Bourbonée, is another

modification of the cross flory ; only its limbs are terminated
by trefoils or triple buds. It is seen, with a glory at the
intersections, among the badges on the Bayeux tapestry.
Besides these there is a cross triparted fleury. Edmondson
says it is " composed for four fleurs-de-lis, conjoined and united
in the centre fess point." The bourdonée has its four limbs

PATÉE FLEURY.   PATÉE CONCAVE.   PATÉE INVECTED.

terminated by spherical excrescences, ornamented with fleurs-
de-lis.

The cross patée, the distinguishing badge of the Knight
Templars, is a cross whose four limbs expand at the extremities, and whose outer edges are flat. The cross is a favourite
as an ornamental emblem on crowns and other regalia, and
also as the badge of many orders of knighthood. There are

PATÉE, FITCHY AT   CROSS FORMÉE OR PATÉE
EACH POINT.   THROUGHOUT.

many modifications of this form. It is sometimes ornamented
with a pearl on each flat end, when it is termed a cross patée-
pomettée ; and sometimes with a fleur-de-lis, when it is
termed patée-fleury. Then there is the cross patée-concave,
with the extremity of each of its limbs curving slightly in-

wards ; patée-convex, with the extremities rounded outwards ; patée-crenellée, with the extremities ornamented
with embattlements ; patée with an engrail at each point,
with a slight indentation at the point or extremity of each
limb ; patée-fitchée at each point, or a cross patée with a
spike terminating each limb ; and patée voided in the foot
in the shape of a V reversed. But the most strange shape
given to this cross is termed a cross patée conjoined and
annulated in the dexter and sinister bases ; it is really four
stripes formed into a square, the angles ornamented with
two wedge-like projections, and the lower conjunctions of
the stripes are pierced by circular holes. The cross patée

CROSS RECERCELÉE
VOIDED, OR ENTRAILED.

ought never to touch the edges of the
shield, but there is a modification of
this cross, whose outline
is rather more curved
and whose edges in-
variably touch the
shield ; it is called a
cross formée. Guillim
specially mentions a
cross recercelée, which,

CROSS
RECERCELÉE.

however, appears to be nothing more than a cross formée-
voided.

The cross potent, of Jerusalem renown, had its four limbs
of equal dimensions, terminated by crutch-like ornaments.

CROSS POTENT.

There are variations. It is termed a cross
potent-crossed when each limb, in addition to
the crutch-like ornament, has a transverse bar.
It undergoes further changes under the name
of potent-rebated, when part of the crutch-
shaped object is removed from one side of each
limb ; potent quadrate (or cross of St. Chad) ;
potent-double fitchée and rebated. Edmondson also mentions a cross potent fleury, fleurs-de-lis being placed at
each end, and some heralds a cross potent rebated in four
points.

The four limbs of the Maltese cross, celebrated as the

badge of the Knights of Malta, expand, and terminate in eight points. These eight points were said to be symbolical of the eight Beatitudes.

The cross-crosslet has its four limbs crossed near the ends by thin bars. It is sometimes mounted on three steps, and

POTENT QUADRATE.   POTENT DOUBLE FITCHY AND REBATED.   POTENT FLEURS-DE-LIS.

MALTESE.   CROSS-CROSSLET.   CROSS CROSSLET PATÉE.

PATRIARCHAL CROSS.   CROSS OF LORRAINE.

is then termed a cross-crosslet Calvary; it is also borne as a cross-crosslet-patée.

The patriarchal cross has two, and sometimes three or four, horizontal bars at the top; it is often formed into a patriarchal cross-crosslet, and sometimes into a patriarchal cross-crosslet-patée. The well-known " White cross of Lorraine " was a patriarchal cross, but with the longer bar placed as near the base as the shorter one is near the top. It was adopted as the badge of the Holy League during the reign of Henry III of France. The very peculiar shape of this cross gave rise to the following unpleasant verses, which were sung by the opponents of the Holy League :

"Mais, dite mois, que sinifie
Que les Ligeurs ont double croix ? "
"C'est q'en la Ligue on crucifie
Jésus Christ encore une fois."

It is now used as the badge of the international organisation for the suppression of tuberculosis.

POMEL.

The opinions of the old heralds are very much divided about the definition of, or difference between, the cross pomel and the cross pomettée. Some have held that they are both the same. Guillim calls a cross with its ends ornamented with round balls a cross pomel ; Edmondson follows his example, and he calls a cross ornamented with double balls a cross pomettée.

URDEE.

The pointed cross has the extremities of its four limbs shaped into sharp points, and is termed by Edmondson urdée. Guillim mentions a star cross ; it differs from the cross fitchy at all points, in its limbs being straight instead of forming sharp points.

The cross nowy has round projections at the angles formed by the conjunction of the limbs.

A cross quadrate has its centre square instead of round.

CROSS NOWY.

CROSS FUSIL.

CROSS FUSIL REBATED.

The extremities of the cross urdee are ornamented by diamond-shaped objects ; Edmondson calls it cross fusil at each point, and he further terms it a cross fusil rebated, when the tips of the diamond-shaped charges are cut off.

The cross raguly has large dents in it, evenly cut, but slanting downwards, and opposite to this indentation is a similarly shaped projection, slanting upwards. The upper limb has one indentation on its dexter side, and one projection on its sinister side ; the lower limb one projection on its dexter, one indentation on its sinister side ; the dexter horizontal limb has one projection on its upper line, and one indentation on its lower line ; the sinister limb one indentation on its upper outline, and one projection on its lower line.

COLCHESTER : TWO STAVES RAGULY IN CROSS (OR CROSSWISE).

Long cross raguly and trunked, so called by Gerard Leigh, Boswell and Edmondson, is termed a cross portant by Holmes.

AVELLANCE.

The avellance cross is formed by a round ball at the conjunction of the four limbs ; each limb is somewhat bell-shaped with a ragged outline at the extremities of the three points. There is also a cross-double avellance.

The cross crescented has its four limbs ornamented by crescents.

The cross clechée is formed of spear-like ornaments. Edmondson, in his "Complete Body of Heraldry," gives the drawing of a cross termed "nowy, grady, conjoined, and fitchée in the foot" ; it is a cross whose four limbs are terminated by two steps, or degrees as they are generally termed in heraldry ; each transverse bar is further ornamented by an oval projection, and the lower limb, beneath the two degrees, is fitchy.

Cross nowed lozengy, is also mentioned by Edmondson.

The cross tron-ornée is a French charge ; it is a Greek

cross cut into five pieces, each part being placed in such a way
as to leave a part of the field visible between.

The cross barbed has its limbs terminated by arrow-heads ;
it is sometimes emblazoned cramponée and tournée, but
Edmondson gives the last name to a totally different cross,
one not unlike the cross fourchée.

A cross double parted or triparted, sometimes termed
crosses of two or three endorses, is formed of either two or
three horizontal and an equal number of perpendicular
stripes, placed in the form of the cross ; sometimes the
double-parted cross has the additional term fretty attached
to it ; in which case the bars are interlaced with each other.

CROSS TRIPARTED.   TRIPARTED FLEURY.

Gerard Leigh mentions a curious cross which he terms a
cross entrailed ; he says it should always be sable, and no
thicker than the stroke of a pen ; the extremities of each
limb are terminated by three loops.

The cross masculy-pometty is formed of four quadrangular links conjoined in the fess point, and each link at three
of its angles bears a circular ball. Guillim says it is a French
cross, and calls it a *croix clechée*. The famous Toulouse
cross, of the Counts of Toulouse, was a cross " vidée, clechée
et pomettée." The Pisan cross is similar, but not voided.

Both Guillim and Gibbon mention another French cross,
termed a *croix de quatre pieces de vaire appointée* ; it is
formed of four of those shield-like objects used in heraldry to
represent the fur termed vair.

The cross moussue, or rounded, is a cross whose limbs,
instead of being cut straight, are all rounded.

ARMS OF CARDINAL WOLSEY, HAMPTON COURT PALACE.

A cross pandell, or spindle, is formed with four elongated globes.

Degraded or degreed and conjoined is a cross mentioned by Edmondson.

A cross cornished and fleury, sometimes termed cornished, is a plain cross with its four limbs terminated like columns, and ornamented with fleurs-de-lis; there is another cross somewhat resembling this one, termed a cross capital. There is yet another architectural

cross, if one may use the term, which is ornamented with scrolls and is called a cross cotised.

The cross thunder, or thunderbolt, is formed of two heraldic thunderbolts placed crosswise, but with the wings left out.

Of crosses ornamented with letters of the alphabet we have two : the cross on each limb a Saxon B, and a long cross on a ball, the top ornamented with a P. Both of these were probably adopted as rebuses on the names, or titles, of the original bearers.

The cross fer de fourchette is merely a Greek cross with curved iron rests, formerly used for resting firelocks, fixed to its ends. But fourchée is like a moline with the ends cut off. The cross couped with an annulet

FOURCHÉE.

at each end, is a plain cross ornamented with rings ; this cross has a modification termed a cross annulated and re-

CROSS MOLINE OR
MILLRINE.

CROSS MOLINE.

CROSS
ANCHORED.

bated ; and again a cross annuly and fretted with a ring, which latter has a small ring entwined with the annulets which terminate the four limbs. It will be noticed that many crosses owe their distinct classification, as separate crosses, merely to the ornaments which they bear at each extremity. The strangest of these is the cross gringollée, or guivrée, whose four limbs are each ornamented with two snakes' heads, one looking to the right and the other to the left.

Perhaps, however, one of the most singular shapes ever given to the cross is that represented by the lambeaux. It is an old device, and displays a curious combination of the

CROSS
LAMBEAUX.

Latin and patée crosses with the label. The upper portion of the cross is shaped like a cross patée, with its lower limb quite straight, until it terminates in a label of three points. One of the old heralds, Sylvanus Morgan, gives the following quaint account of it. It has, he says, " a great deal of mystery in relation to the top, whereon the first born Son of God did suffer, sending out three streams (of light ?) from His hands, feet, and sides." There is also a cross lambeaux in all four limbs, when a label of three points terminates each limb.

Some of the prettiest heraldic crosses are the floral ones ; they are generally of the Greek, though sometimes of the Latin shape. There are the oak crosses, formed of oak leaves and acorns ; the laurel cross ; and cross formed of ears of wheat and barley. Then we have crosses formed of roses, either red or white ; and lily crosses. Crosses are frequently angled with acorns, leaves, ears of corn, passion nails, and fleurs-de-lis. A cross fruitage is formed of cup-like pods, bursting and displaying a quantity of grapes ; the stems are joined together in the fess point by an annulet. The cross of triangles was probably intended to repre-

CROSS   PATONCE,
ACORNED AT EACH
ANGLE.

sent a cross formed of thorns, broken off from the branch, and the spikes stuck into the bases of others, just as children are so fond of making wreaths and other ornaments with the thorns of roses and brambles. Roses and other charges when five in number are constantly borne either in cross or in saltire. The quatrefoil is mentioned by some heralds as a cross of leaves.

When the lower limb of any of these crosses is represented as having a spike, which is of constant occurrence in heraldry,

it is termed a cross fitchy or fitchée. These crosses were used by pilgrims while on their long journeys, when they could not avail themselves of village churches or market crosses; they therefore stuck their little crosses in the ground as a preliminary to their

FITCHY.

CROSS CROSSLET FITCHY.

daily devotions; the soldiers of the Crusading armies are said to have made use of their swords for this purpose. Of this practice we have an instance in the brave Chevalier Bayard, who, when he received his death wound on the battlefield of Romagnans, and perceiving that no priest was forthcoming to perform the last offices, ordered his attendant to stick the pointed end of his long knightly sword into the turf, and thus improvise a small altar.

Crosses are either simply fitchy, when the lower limb is sharpened into a point, or fitchy in the foot, as a cross patée

CROSS CROSSLET FITCHY AT FOOT.   DOUBLE FITCHY AND REBATED.

fitchy in the foot, when the lower limb is of its proper shape, but with a spike affixed to it. A plain cross may be fitchy at all points, double fitchy at all points, and sometimes the last cross has the tips of the spikes cut off, and is then termed rebated. Besides these there is a cross used by French heralds termed a cross " fourchée a douze pointes," which is a cross fitchée at all points. Guillim also mentions that he saw in a French work a cross called " croix à seizes pointes," each limb being fitchy of four points.

Componée, or gobony, is a term applied to a cross, or any other ordinary, when it is formed of a row of small squares, alternately of colour and metal, the tinctures always being mentioned. Roundels are frequently borne in the form of the cross, each roundel touching the other, and these charges are emblazoned as a cross beyantée, platée, etc., according to their tinctures. There are also crosses fusily and lozengy, being composed respectively of acute and blunt lozenges. But the cross lozengy must not be confounded with the cross lozenge, which is a cross composed of four lozenges, placed with the four acute angles, meeting in the middle or fess point.

VOIDED.   SQUARE PIERCED.   VOIDED AND COUPED.

A cross masculy is formed of quadrangular links, the links formerly used in chain armour. A cross annuly, or a cross of annulets interlaced, is formed of circular links. Crosses may also be voided, that is to say, only the mere outline of he cross is drawn, showing the field through it ; the voiding may be in the shape of the pale, the fess, or in the shape of some other cross, but when merely emblazoned voided it is voided of its own shape. A circular hole is often made at the junction of the four limbs ; this is termed pierced, or, if the hole be square, square-pierced ; but if the whole of the intersecting part of the cross is removed, it is termed quarterly pierced. This last forms a field checky of nine pieces, and is called by French heralds equipollé.

A cross may be divided per pale, per fess, or per bend, each half being of different tinctures ; it may also be quartered. A cross divided per pale, per fess, and per saltire, is termed a cross quarterly-quartered. Sir George Mackenzie gives as the arms of Glendening of that ilk : per cross, argent, and sable ; a cross parted per cross, indented, and counterchanged.

Fimbriated is a cross with a border of a different colour ; for instance, the cross of St. George in the " Union Jack " is a cross gule fimbriated argent. The badge of the Knights of St. Iago of Spain is a red cross patonce fitchy, fimbriated argent, with a silver escallop shell. If the limbs of a plain or long cross do not touch the sides of the shield, it is termed indifferently couped or humettée, if cut off with a smooth edge ; but if with a jagged edge, erased or rompu. The rounded or moussue cross is a cross humettée, only instead of the ends being cut straight

BADGE OF
KNIGHTS OF
ST. IAGO.

they are rounded off. It must be remembered that these terms, couped and humettée, can only refer to the plain or long crosses, or to the saltire. The term crusily is applied to a shield whose field is strewn with crosses. The term cantonnée is used to describe a cross placed between four crosses or four other charges. Engoulé is a term employed when the extremities of a cross, saltire, or other ordinary, enter the mouths of lions or any other wild beast.

CROSSES OF
JERUSALEM,
CANTONNÉE.

One cross may be charged with another of the same or of a different form. [1] Besides being charged with different

CROSS MOLINE IN PALE
AND PATÉE IN FESS.

[1] There is a general confusion with regard to crosses *charged*, *voided*, and *fimbriated*. A cross is always voided of the field. The border of a cross fimbriated is very narrow ; much more so than the edges of a *voided* cross. When a cross is *charged with another* the charge is always less than one-third of the size of the first, and, generally, both crosses are of a different tincture to the field.

suffered martyrdom on a cross of this shape. It has always
been a favourite charge with the heralds, and is the national
badge both of Scotland and Ireland. An old legend attributes the origin of this cross as the Scottish national badge
to the fact of its having miraculously appeared to the King of
the Picts (Lowlanders) on the eve of the battle in which his
people gained a signal victory over the Northumbrians.

It is largely employed in Scottish heraldry, either borne
singly, in pairs, by threes, or the shield covered with them ;

SALTIRE.   SALTIRE BOTONY.   SALTIRE CROSSLET.

SALTIRE CROSSLET   SALTIRE CROSSLET   SALTIRE MOLINE.
FLEURY.   PATÉE.

in the latter case the proper heraldic term is, a field semée of
saltires. When more than one saltire is blazoned they are
always couped, straight across, not diagonally, but as they
are always borne thus, it is unnecessary to blazon them as
couped. This rule, of course, does not apply in a case where
a single saltire is borne couped, for in such a case it is abso-
lutely necessary to mention it, otherwise it would be taken
for granted that the ends of the saltire touch the edges of
the shield.

The term salterwise is applied to two objects borne in the

form of the saltire ; unless otherwise blazoned the object
in sinister bend should always be uppermost ; five charges
placed two, one, two are blazoned in saltire ; a shield may
be party per saltire.

Saltires patée, pomettée, fleury, potentée, and crossed,
assume the peculiar forms or ornaments of the crosses bearing
these different names.

Saltires may also be formed of the different lines of partition,
and Guillim mentions a saltire-raguly, which is the cross of
Burgundy.

A saltire of two tinctures divided into eight portions is
termed a saltire quarterly quartered.

Four chains are sometimes borne in saltire, each being
fixed to an annulet in the centre.

A saltire joined in the base has a horizontal band joining
the two lower limbs of the saltire.   Robert de Bruce (temp.
Henry III) bore : or, a saltire gules and a chief of the second ;
while the most ancient branch of the Nevils bore (as early
as the reign of Edward II) : gules, a saltire argent.

The pall is formed by the upper portion of a saltire conjoined to the lower part of the pale, and in fact resembles
very closely the letter Y.   It is a Roman Catholic ecclesiastical vestment.   The Pope on raising a priest to the dignity
of archbishop always sends him a pall, and he is not, according
to the strict etiquette of the Church, qualified to perform
any archiepiscopal duties until he has been duly invested with
the pall.   It was first used in 1152.

In heraldry it is seldom used, except for bishops' sees or
ecclesiastical communities.   The arms of the archbishopric of
Canterbury are : azure, an episcopal staff in pale, or, ensigned
with a cross pattée, argent, surmounted by a pall of the
second, edged, and fringed, or charged with four crosses-
pattée fitchée, sable.   The arms of the archbishopric of
Dublin are the same as those of Armagh, only the pall is
charged with five crosses instead of four.

The cross tau, or St. Anthony's Cross, closely resembles
the Greek letter tau, from which it derives its name.   Besides
the plain cross tau there is one termed cross-tau ends con-

3

vexed, and graded ; it is mounted on three steps, and the two
ends of the horizontal bar are terminated by crescents.

CROSS TAU RAGULY.   CROSS TAU PATÉE.

The cross portrate is a French charge, and held an important
place in the list of their heraldic charges. It is a saltire
with the upper portion of the bend dexter cut off.

La Colombière, Edmondson and others mention a charge
which they call a cross potence, but which Holmes affirms
should be termed a Saxon F, which it certainly resembles.
Holmes also states that it forms the insignia of the bishopric
of Chemin, a province of Saxony.

CHAPTER IV

ANIMALS: I. FOUR-FOOTED BEASTS

IN the early days of heraldry, when each knight could decorate his shield with the emblems that pleased him best, many chose for the principal charges on their coats-of-arms some of those animals most renowned for bravery. Therefore the lion, the leopard, the eagle, the wild boar, and, at a much later date, dragons and griffins, were widely adopted as distinguishing badges. But as sovereign princes in nearly every case chose one of the warrior beasts, to avoid confusion, gradually extraordinary posture, contour and colouring crept into the art of blazoning.

The lion, chosen at an early date by the kings of England, was perhaps the animal most highly esteemed by heraldic authorities; it is, therefore, hardly astonishing to find that it has undergone many curious alterations. The lion is borne in fifteen postures:

(1) "Rampant," erect on its hind legs, going from sinister side to dexter, its head being in profile, and its tail erect and nearly touching its back. (2) "Rampant-guardant," erect on its hind legs, and full faced. (3) "Rampant-regardant," erect on its hind legs, its head in profile looking backwards. (4) "Passant," walking past in profile, its right front paw held up, and its tail reflexed over the back. (5) "Passant-guardant," walking past, full-faced, right leg lifted, and tail reflexed over back. (6) "Passant-regardant," in the same position as the last two, only with its head in profile looking backwards. (7) "Standant," with all four paws on the ground; it is generally emblazoned full-faced. (8) "Saliant," or in the act of springing forward; there is really but very

little difference between saliant and passant, but the former has its two front legs in the air. (9) "Sejeant," seated on its haunches, its head in profile, and front paws on the ground. (10) "Sejeant-affronté," sitting upright, full-faced, with its front legs held straight out on either side. (11) "Couchant,"

RAMPANT.   RAMPANT GUARDANT.   RAMPANT REGARDANT.

PASSANT.   PASSANT GUARDANT.

PASSANT REGARDANT.   STANDANT OR STATANT.

lying down, its head erect, and tail beneath it. (12) "Dormant," with its head resting on its front paws. (13) "Coward" or "cowé," the same posture as standant, its head held rather lower, and its tail between its legs. (14) "Rampant-combatant," two lions "rampant-passant" placed face to face. (15) " Rampant-adossé," or " addorsed," two lions "rampant-passant," placed back to back.

In accordance with fairly early practice a lion is always given a tongue and claws of a different tincture to that of its body. If a golden or silvern lion is placed on a blue, black or green field the tongue and claws are red ; if on a red field, they are blue. Sometimes, though this is rare, a golden lion on a black field has a tongue and claws of silver. On the other hand, the red lion has a blue tongue and claws whenever possible, or failing that they are gold or silver ; and the blue lion has red tongue and claws. Such lions, and other beasts so treated, are said to be " langued and armed " of the special tincture. Unless otherwise described, the tails of lions are borne reflexed over their backs, and in mediæval examples the tails are often nearly twice as long as the whole body. This is the case in the very spiritedly carved lions on the coat of Edmund of Langley, Earl of Cambridge and Duke of York, fifth son of Edward III, as seen carved on his tomb in the church of King's Langley, Hertfordshire. But the tails may be " nowed " (tied in a knot), " fourchée " (bifurcated towards the tip) or borne double, as in the well-known Bohemian beast.

A lion may be borne dismembered, as in the coat of Maitland (or, a lion dismembered, gules) when the head, four limbs and tail are severed from the body, a thin line of the field showing between. Akin to this is the demi-lion, the upper part, which is used not only as a crest, but also as a charge, a striking and suggestive example being the demi-Scottish lion of augmentation on the chief of Thomas Howard, Duke of Norfolk (see Chapter

TRI-CORPATE.

XII). Shadows of lions have appeared on German shields, a mere outline in a darker shade of the field being drawn. Then there are bi- and tri-corpate lions. In the first instance the two bodies are borne salient from dexter and sinister, the first " contourné," so that they face each

other, the two necks being joined to a single full-faced
head ; in the second, the bodies radiate " en pairle," to
dexter chief, sinister chief and base, the necks meeting in a
single head in fess point. On the Continent lions are seen
wearing helmets and even, as in the case of the Brittany
Hattes, with the head smothered in blue cloth, while the red
lion of Reinach, which apparently had been dancing, for it is
contourné, has its head covered by a tight-fitting blue sack.
It is tempting to speculate whether one ought to read some
political allusion in these quaint devices (as with the knotty
club, and the smoothing plane which the Dukes of Burgundy
and Bourbon added to their escutcheons, to make manifest
their keen desire to be at each other's throats), or whether
they should be regarded as merely grotesques. Such humorous
renderings of heraldic compositions were common enough at
tournaments, when knights desired to preserve their *incog-
nito* while hinting at their personalities or their hidden motives.
Some of these may (as the " tenants " or supporters undoubtedly were), have been permanently adopted by the
knight or his squire. Many odd additions unquestionably
are errors introduced by careless painters and ignorantly
prepetuated, but others have real meaning. Thus it is with
the blue cape semée with golden fleurs-de-lis, which we find on
the rampant red lion within an orle of plates on a field gules,
belonging to the Cardilacs. Vulson de la Colombière tells
us this was a personal honour bestowed by the King of
France for services rendered ; but whether the services were
such as are performed *sous le manteau* tradition is silent.

With us it is common to see lions holding swords, lances,
flags, human heads and other trifles between their paws.
In French heraldry they may be seen having thrown aside
the trappings of war, and, if not having converted swords
into ploughshares, at all events taken up implements of hus-
bandry. For we find that Athenor bore : azure, a lion rampant with human head, coiffed with a broad-brimmed and
tall crowned hat, holding a hoe, or. Lions' heads (with the
neck) and faces (without the neck, showing the mask only),
also " gambs " or " jambs " (legs) and paws are borne, as

well as plain tails. An English bearing is that of Corke : sable, three lions' tails, argent. When a number of small lions are figured on a coat they are blazoned " lioncels." In olden phraseology the word " leopard " was generally applied to lions passant-guardant, though there was nothing in the drawing to justify the name. Later the lion passant-guardant came to be called a " lion-leopardé," but it was merely a term applied to the beasts in a special attitude, and had no other significance. This is important to remember as in old writings the English cognisance is constantly referred to as the golden leopards. As we shall see presently, these kings of the beasts have also been converted into dragon-lions and marine lions.

Among the famous lions of chivalry are the golden lions passant-guardant of England ; the red lion rampant of Scotland ; the silver lions passant of the native Princes of North and South Wales ; and the black lion rampant of the Griffiths, Princes of Cardigan. Then there are the white lion of the Earls of March ; the gold lion statant with extended tail, the badge of the Percys ; the Howards' gold lion statant-guardant with extended tail, with a ducal coronet of silver; the Lacy Earls of Lincoln purple lion rampant, and others. Going abroad we find the valiant winged lion of Venice, with its nimbus about its head, its paw on the table of laws. This, of course, is the Biblical lion of St. Mark. The lion of Flanders is black and rampant ; that of Bohemia was silver, and also rampant, with double tail proudly whisking at its back ; that of Gelders was rampant or, crowned gules ; that of Leon, rampant and originally purple, though it has long since become red ; while the Luxemburg beast is barry of gold and red.

Heraldic leopards belong to the early sixteenth century ; the spots are represented by a number of roundels, often of varied tinctures, powdered over the body. The " leopard's face " (a lion's face without the mane) is often met with. This mask of the leopard is constantly blazoned as " jessant-de-lis," that is shown with the tail of a fleur-de-lis coming out of its mouth, and the lobes showing up behind. To make matters worse the leopard's head "jessant-de-lis" is as likely as not to be borne reversed, that is upside down, as in the arms of the See of Hereford.

Heraldic tigers have the bodies of lions and the heads of wolves, and are usually spitting fire. It was supposed to be proper to depict them as statant, gazing into a mirror on the ground. This was in reference to the old traveller's tale that when a leopard was deprived of its whelps, it was well to place a mirror near the den, so that the mother might be attracted by her reflection, and stay either to admire herself or to puzzle out the ghostly presence of a possible rival. The striped tiger was introduced into heraldry by adventurous travellers and successful soldiers of the eighteenth and nineteenth centuries, who had won fame and fortune in India.

JESSANT-DE-LIS.

FOXES IN SALTIRE, OR RAMPANT
COUNTER RAMPANT.

A lynx and a catamount, or wild cat, are much alike, spitting fire, and being adorned on head and limbs with tufts of fur.

Bears are also very old symbols, as witness the rampant bear and ragged staff of the Earls of Warwick, the beast having, it is alleged, been derived from Urso d'Abitot, one of the Conqueror's barons. The bear is also seen on the shield of Berne City, this being a canting coat. Polar bears are the result of eighteenth and nineteenth century exploring work.

Wolves naturally play a big part. They are shown " rampant," " passant," " courant," " vorant " (devouring prey), " ravisant " (carrying it off), and in many other positions ; while their heads are favourite charges. It is significant that the ravisant wolf is often seen on Spanish shields. Wolves

LION PASSANT.   JACOBEAN FIRE-BACK.

40]

are borne as warlike or sporting symbols, but quite often as
punning allusion to the wearers, the Wolves, Lovels, and so
on, as will be seen more at length on referring to Chapter XIV.

The fox is another creature of the chase largely used, either
whole, or his mask, or his brush. A fox rampant, with a
hood on its back in which there is a goose, is to be seen on a
German coat-of-arms, that of the Schaden von Leipolds. It
is strongly reminiscent of the satirical Gothic church carvings.

Oxen are shown passant, though they are occasionally
rampant. The ox's head and his scalp with horns are also
borne. These may represent great landed interests, but more
frequently they bear some canting allusion, as in the ox on
the blue water on the shield of Oxford City. The winged,
nimbus crowned bull of St. John is also among the heraldic
charges, and his prototype may be found in the great symbolic
winged bulls of Nineveh. A shaggy maned buffalo is seen on
the shield of Manitoba.

Sheep also partake of mixed symbolism, now representing
agricultural or commercial interest, and anon religious senti-
ment. In the former case we may have either the live sheep
(sometimes bearing a sprig in its mouth, as in the case of
Bolton, where the sheep has a sprig of the fructed cotton-

LEEDS : A FLEECE BANDED.

plant, to represent the woollen and cotton industries), or the
fleece, that is, the undressed skin with head and hoofs. The
golden fleece of classic tradition was the cherished emblem of
a noble order of knighthood founded in connection with the
Holy Roman Empire, and now bestowed both by the King

themselves were merely symbolical of the forestry and hunting privileges. Anciently the arms were : azure, a tower,
triple towered, argent. The other emblems came later to
record civic privileges.

The rabbit is termed a " conie," the badger a " brock " or
a " gray " ; the hedgehog a " herison "; then there are goats
and goats' heads, asses and asses' heads. Hares are not unknown. Indeed, that of Cleland, saliant with a hunting-horn
round its neck, is found on many a noble coat, or as a crest,
owing to family alliances. Other musical hares are those of
FitzErcald, co. Derby : argent, three hares sejant gules,
playing upon bagpipes, or. Hopwell bore the same arms, only
both hares and bagpipes were red. Sir William Mauleverer
(temp. Edward III) bore : argent, three leverers gules.

The stag is said to be at " gaze " when it is standing still,
" trippant " when passing, " courant " or " at speed "
when running. When its antlers are of a different tincture
to that of the animal it is said to be " attired," just the same
as the lion, or other savage beast, is said to be " armed "
when its claws, teeth, or beak are of a different tincture. The
antlers are sometimes borne alone, and are then known as
" attires," while a branch is a " tyne." The male is called
a " hart " and the female a " hind." A young stag is termed
a " girl." Within the last three hundred years the reindeer
and moose have been introduced from
Canada, and the gnu, springbok and gems-
bok from Africa.

STAG'S HEAD
CABOCHED.

" Caboched " is a term applied to the
head of any animal when it is represented, either full-faced or without a
neck. If the neck is shown with a clean
cut, it is said to be " couped," but if with
a jagged edge, then it is " erased " ;
terms which apply to all members of
human beings, the lower animals, plants,
or inanimate objects, when respectively clean cut or torn
off. Any beast of prey lying down with its head held up
is said to be " couchant," but a stag or other beast of chase

GOATS' HEADS ERASED (CORDWAINERS' GUILD, DURHAM).

44]

in this position is said to be " lodged " ; a wild beast eating
its food is termed "vorant "; " vulned " is a term applied
to an animal, or part of an animal, dripping with blood ; an
animal " courant " is running ; " saliant," it is about to
spring forward ; " respecting " is applied to other animals,
except lions and other beasts of prey, when they are placed
face to face ; in this position beasts of prey are said to be
" combatant." A tortoise walking is said to be " gradiant."

All beasts deprived of their tails are said to be " defamed " ;
if the tails are borne between their legs they are termed
" couée " or " coward." If an or-
dinary is borne over them, they are
said to be " debruised." But all
animals may be crowned, and they
may also be "gorged," either with
a wreath of leaves or flowers, a collar
or a coronet about their necks. If
flames issue from their mouths or
nostrils, they are " incensed " or
" inflamed." Beasts and birds are
always supposed to face to the dexter, if otherwise they are said to be
" contourné," or reversed.

GORGED WITH COLLAR
FLORY COUNTER FLORY.

While beasts and birds of prey are
said to be "armed" when their teeth, tusks, beaks, claws
and talons are of a different tincture to that of their bodies,
under these conditions wild boars and elephants are more
frequently said to be "tusked." Hoofed animals are said
to be " hoofed " or " unguled " of any special tincture. A
horse, unicorn or lion with a mane of a different tincture
to the body is said to be " crined " of a special colour ; a
term which also applies to the hair of the human head.

It is to be noted that while many beasts and birds were
introduced into heraldry, either as representatives of those
virtues specially admired in warriors, or as symbols of the
pleasures and jealously guarded privileges of the chase, a
goodly number appear to have been adopted mainly, if not
solely, because their names suggested allusions to the patrony-

was the type adopted by Napoleon I and by his nephew, Napoleon III. The naturalistic character is carried still further in the American national eagle, which is essentially a bird of prey, with its neck depressed, the head pushed forward, the beak open, the wings outspread, and the whole attitude showing readiness for a pounce. It grasps thunderbolts in

EAGLE FROM TRAJAN'S COLUMN, ROME.

the form of forked lightning, in its talons. The Teutonic eagle, on the other hand, is purely a creature of convention. It is attenuated, angular and rugged in outline, with long neck, prominent open beak, lolling tongue, large eyes, plumed legs, with great talons ; its wings are ragged, the flight feathers appearing singly, not massed together, and its tail is a long projection, decorated with foliated scroll-work, often quite architectural in character. A modified form of this may be seen in the north choir-aisle of Westminster Abbey, on a shield of Emperor Frederick II (*temp*. Henry III).

BEDFORD: AN EAGLE WITH WINGS ABAISÉ.

Displayed eagles have their wings open and elevated, sometimes the tips being carried on a level with the head and then ending horizontally, the pinions being carried erect, the wings spread fan-wise, with the feathers projecting above the head. The term " abaisé " is applied when the wings are spread, but the feathers point downwards. The Apostolic eagle has a nimbus round its head, and is the symbol of St. John.

The double-headed eagle of the Holy Roman Empire is sometimes crowned, sometimes bears the nimbus. This

DOUBLE-HEADED HITTITE EAGLE FROM CAPPADOCIA.

double-headed eagle is now used by the Emperors of Austria and of Russia. The dual heads represent dominion over east and west. Prototypes of the double-headed eagles are found in the ancient rock carvings of Cappadocia, where we see double-headed eagles supporting divinities, and in one case clutching a hare in its talons. These were adopted by the Seleuke Turcomans, and through them migrated to Eastern Europe.

DOUBLE-HEADED
HITTITE EAGLE.

A coat-of-arms is often borne on the breast of an eagle (as in the case of Prussia, Austria, Russia and the United States of America), or as we may see it nearer home, in the case of the town of Bedford, occasionally the shield being pendent from a belt held in the beak. Sometimes the outspread

4

wings are also covered with armorial shields, as in the case of Russia and Austria. In early heraldry the eagle was often blazoned as an " erne " or an " alerion." Later the term alerion was applied to small beakless and talonless eagles. The arms of the Duchy of Lorraine are : or, on a bend gules, three alerions abaisé, argent. Legend says that the alerions came to Lorraine through Geoffrey of Bouillon, who when before Jerusalem shot an arrow which slew three strange beakless and feetless birds, which he straightway adopted as his personal cognisance. It is possible that they were indeed arms of assumption, some strange Eastern symbolism taken from the shield of a vanquished leader. Among our famous eagles is the green bird with red beak and talons on the gold shield

EGYPTIAN SACRED VULTURE WITH PLUME SCEPTRES.

of the redoubtable and influential Monthermer. On a Roll of Arms of Henry III, John de Beauchamp is said to bear : sable, an eagle argent armed or. One of the strangest looking of these fowls was on the feudal coat of the Margraf of Moravia : azure, an eagle displayed chequy argent and gules, crowned or. De Ganays, of Burgundy, who derive from a lawyer stock, bear emblematically : or, an eagle disarmed sable ; for the talons and beak properly belong to the warrior.

In the early days of chivalry hawking was one of the principal pastimes of nobility, and therefore both the hawks and the objects used in hawking were often chosen by those who had special rights of hunting over large extents of forest. Hawks often appear as " belled," " jessed " and " varvelled." The " bell," which is constantly used as a separate charge, is round with a long slit in it ; a piece of metal at the top is pierced by a hole, through which the " jess," or leather thong, is passed ; and so fastened to the leg of the hawk.

" Varvels " are rings attached to the leather thongs. Hawking has contributed two other names to heraldry : the hawk's " lure " or two wings joined with a thong, to which is tied a ring ; and " nowed," a term used when the thongs are knotted.

Swans, being royal birds of the chase, and also having a long and illustrious record in the legendary tales of most nations, more especially those of the North, where they appear as carriers of human souls to Thor's Valhalla, play an important part in heraldry. The swan is essentially a bird of chivalry, of queens, and knight-errantry. It is generally white or silver, with black beak and red legs, and is then blazoned " proper." In our history the most famous swan is the white one, gorged with a golden coronet, with chain attached, passing over its back, which belonged to the de Bohuns. They derived it from the Mandevilles, Earls of Essex, who got it from their forebears, the Fitzswans, whose progenitor came over from Normandy with Duke William in 1066. So that this is the real Norseman's mystic messenger from the outer world.

ARMS OF THE GUILD OF
MUSICIANS, LONDON.

The de Bohuns transmitted their swan to the Lancastrian branch of the Plantagenets, the Staffords and many other noble houses. Swan (*obit.* 1487) bore : azure, a fess between three swans argent. Black swans of Australia, with their red beaks and legs, are now occasionally seen. A " swan's neck " includes both head and neck.

Another equally long-pedigreed feathered messenger from the regions of shadow was the raven, usually styled a " corbie." These solemn sable birds, meeting in conclave and often acting in concert after such " conferences," have always been held in awe. In certain parts of India they are the

preferred refuges of human souls, while to several American
Indian tribes, west of the Rockies, the Great Raven, creator
of the world, was their progenitor. Our mid-German Arian
ancestors venerated the birds, so did the Danes, as certainly
did the Celts of the western parts of our land. A raven standard
was borne by the Danes who invaded
our shores in 787, and fell to Alfred at
the battle of Westbury some hundred
years later. It was always prominent
in battle, and a bringer of omens.
While a raven helped the Roman
Valerius against the Gauls, causing
him, so legend says, to assume the
name of Corvus (though that was
probably a reminiscence of totemism),

CITY OF CANTERBURY.

a flock of them accompanied Owain Urien to the wars,
and in later times they flew about Wales, declaring that
Gwffydd ap Rhys ap Tudor would ultimately prevail and
become Prince of Wales. To this day, the vanished King
Arthur circles about our islands and Brittany in the form of
a gigantic raven, awaiting the opportune time to reappear
as ruler of the United Brittanies. With such a record of
warfaring and wisdom, the raven was always much favoured
by heralds, and is specially prominent as a crest. Griffith
ap Rhys ap Uryan had for badge a black raven on a white
quatrefoil, shipped and leaved gold. Thomas de Corbet
(*temp.* Henry III), following the example of Valerius, took
unto himself : or, two corbies, sable.

Swallows, with their long bifurcated tails and long wings,
are messengers from afar off, who have been largely used.
The martin, a smaller bird, usually borne " closed," is called
a " martlet." This last has gradually been deprived of its
beak and legs. Arundell of Wardour bore : sable, six swallows
(3, 2, 1) argent.

The ostrich came to us early from the East, being brought
back by the Crusaders. It was regarded as a symbol of
endurance and martial ardour, partly no doubt owing to its
swiftness of foot and combativeness at certain seasons, but

COQ GAULOIS.

more particularly because of its hardiness and power of long
abstinence, combined with healthy digestive powers. This
latter peculiarity gave rise to the legend that it could live on
iron, hence the practice of heralds of showing it bearing a
Passion nail (emblem of the Church Militant), a horseshoe
(itself an old symbol of religion, but more particularly assumed
as a reminder of knightly prowess on horseback), or a key
(a symbol at once of religious and temporal power). How
it became intimately connected with England will be discussed in another chapter, when dealing with the plumes of
the Princes of Wales. Allied to the Eastern ostrich are the
later introduced emu and apterix of Australia.

After the eagle and hawk the birds most commonly used
in heraldry are the pelican, the
peacock and the cock. The
pelican is generally borne with
its wings open and placed back
to back ; or in her nest feeding
her young with her own blood,
flowing from a self-inflicted
wound on her breast, when she
is said to be " in her piety."
It is a religious emblem. We
also have storks, the bringers
of children ; and cranes. The
latter are nearly always depicted as standing on one leg,

PELICAN IN HER PIETY.

holding a stone in the other. This stone, travellers said,
was held so that if the bird should nap, it would fall and
waken the sentinel. Nevertheless, the crane is regarded
as the symbol of vigilance. Doves, originally the birds of
Aphrodite and Venus, took men's souls to heaven, hence
their association with the symbolism of the Holy Spirit.
Columball (temp. Richard II) bore : sable, three doves argent,
beaked and membered gules, holding in their beaks sprigs
of olives proper. Obviously allusive alike to the name of the
bearer and the Biblical lesson. They are, indeed, mostly
found in heraldry as an emblem of love and of religious ardour.

On the other hand, the owl, bird of Pallas Athene, and originally bird of death, is associated with worldly wisdom, and was largely allotted as a symbol for clerkly armouries.

The cock, owing to its pugnacity, was always regarded as

COCK CROWNED HEAD, ROMAN
COIN MINTED IN GAUL.

COCK HELMET, COIN MINTED
BY GAULS.

bird of battle, and in war time a white cock with red comb was sacrificed to Mars. On the other hand, it was sacred to Attis, the god of spring and fertility of the Eastern Mediterranean, thus bringing it, with the hen, into the circle of universal symbolism, as the hatchers of the great World Egg. Its wakefulness and matutinal clarion calls, associated with the repentance of St. Peter, made it a favourite Christian symbol, constantly placed on church steeple to call humanity to their duties. In heraldry it appears under its dual nature—a symbol of soldierly courage and of religious aspirations. It appears to have

GNOSTIC COCK-SNAKE GOD.

been associated with the religious cult of the Gauls, for Cæsar tells us that they fought under a cock standard. The bird appears on Gallo-Roman sculpture, and the Romans placed a curious representation of a cock war helmet on coins minted in Gaul. We find it used in national symbolism of the early Bourbons, and it was definitely adopted as the French avian emblem under Louis Philippe. A good representation of the coq Gaulois is given facing page 52, which shows the badge worn on the shako of an officer of the Civic Guards under that monarch. The cock, when its comb, gills, claws, and beak are of a different tincture from the body itself, is said to be " crested," " jelloped," and " armed." Birds possessing no talons are said to be " beaked " and " membered " when their beaks and legs are of a different tincture.

The peacock is generally borne " in its pride," that is to say, full-faced and with tail outspread. It held a high place in Eastern symbolism, as witness the peacock throne of Persia ; the peacock plumes of the Chinese mandarins ; and the peacock fans—wafters away of evil spirits—carried by the attendants of Eastern potentates. It was the bird of rainbow-throned Juno, consort of Jove ; and the rainbow hues of its gorgeous tail brought it within the Christian symbolism of the Resurrection.

Among game birds we have the partridge, the pheasant and the heath cock or moor hen. Partridge bears : gules, on a fess argent between three lions rampant, or, as many partridges proper ; while Saxby, of Kent, has the far prettier shield : vert, a garb between three partridges or ; Faisant : azure, three pheasants or, beaked and membered gules ; Mores : argent, a heath cock (or moor hen) proper, comb and gills gules.

Parrots appear under the name of " popinjays." These steeds of the Hindu cupid, or god of love, were used in heraldry as early as the reign of Henry III. In later centuries they were sometimes employed to commemorate administrative or commercial success in tropical countries. Marmaduk de Twenge (*temp*. Henry III) bore : argent, a fess between three popinjays vert ; and Richard FitzMarmaduk, of the same period : gules, a fess between three popinjays argent, a baton azure over all. Cornish chough is the name of a small bird of the crow tribe, with bluish black plumage, and red beak and legs. It was long a mark of Cornish origin.

Cormorants appear as symbols of sea-power, as in the

arms of Liverpool : argent, a cormorant, sable armed gule, holding in its beak a sprig of laver seaweed, vert. One of the supporters of the national arms of Chile is a condor. David of Llwch prettily bears : azure, three seagulls argent ; and Mewey, co. Devon : gules, three seamews argent, beaked and legged or.

A bird when raising its wings preparatory to flying is said to be " rising "; if flying " volant "; and

LIVERPOOL.

when a bird of prey is represented as devouring its food it is said to be " preying." Sometimes a feather has its quill of a different tincture to itself, in which case it is emblazoned as " quilled " of such a tincture. A bird with wings closed is said to be " close " or " trussed."

PEACOCK IN HIS PRIDE.

CHAPTER VI

FISH, AMPHIBIA, OPHIDIA AND INSECTS

FISH are emblazoned in four principal positions : as " hauriant," in a perpendicular position, the head upwards ; " urinant," also perpendicular, but with the head downwards, as though diving ; " naiant," or swimming horizontally ; and as " embowed," or bent. The dolphin, a very favourite device, is always borne " embowed."

The dolphin was early employed by Asiatics and Greeks as a symbol of maritime power, and by the latter also as emblematic of youth. It was not only placed on the shield of Ulysses in token of his voyages, but was sacred to Apollo. It took the bodies of shipwrecked lovers of music and the gods safely to land, or conveyed their souls to the Fortunate Isles. The Egyptians paid worship to fish and used them as symbols. With them fish were guardians of souls. Two of them, Abtu and Ant, swam before Ra's boat during his nightly voyages through the Underworld of Tuat. In Christian iconogprahy it represents the Resurrection, for the dolphin is beautiful in death, rapidly changing into the colours of the rainbow, that sign of hope. Dolphins are conventionalised figures of a large-headed, finned, cetaceous mammal. On Greek coins and vases they appear as somewhat elongated fish, with beak-like snouts, crested fins at the back of their heads, bifurcated tails, the body slightly bowed, forming a depressed arch from tail to head. A splendid example of two such dolphins may be seen in white on a black circular shield adorning a Greek vase preserved at the British Museum. In symbolism and heraldry they represent sea-power and travel, and so may be seen alike on the shields of sailors, merchants and seaports. They are usually shown " embowed naiant," presenting an undulating outline, the body arched, the snout curved and the tail flat ; the dorsal fin prominent and spiky, being carried from the head almost to the tail ; the pectoral fins small ; the tail bifurcated or triparted. But for crests the favourite attitude is the diving one. They are sometimes borne in saltire and also endorsed. In Continental heraldry the dolphin is often shown " hauriant " as well as bent into a semicircle. It generally appears in this form, as on the quartered coat and as the badge of the former heirs-apparent to the Crown of France, who, from the reign of Charles V to the day of the unhappy son of Louis XVI, derived their title Dauphin, and their insignia of a blue dolphin with red eyes and fins on a gold field, from the ancient county of Viennois, later known as Dauphiné, from the title of Dauphin assumed by its rulers. Both the title and arms are mysterious, for the title was only assumed in 1100 by Guigue IV, and the dolphin did not appear until many years after. It has therefore been conjectured that the arms are allusive to the title, which itself is supposed to have been derived from the Celtic *dal*, (district) *na*, (of the) and *pen* or *pin* (point, hill, head, chief, leader) ; thus the embowed fish stood for district head leader. Twice failure occurred in the male line, though the title and arms were continued. Then Humbert III, last of the third line, sold his county to Philip of France, and the rich district became attached to the throne, and the title passed to the heirs thereof. Dolphins have also long been associated with the county of Devonshire. A dolphin is the crest of the Courtenays, Earls of Devon, and appears on the seal of Catherine of York, wife of Edward IV. It is used as a kind of supporter on the side of the shield. The Courtenays apparently derived it from De Abincis, hereditary sheriffs of Devon, whose heiress the first of the Courtenays to come to England married. A dolphin curled round an anchor or a trident is a venerable symbol, found on Greek vases ; both designs have been incorporated among heraldic emblems, chiefly as crests.

Another, and larger, denizen of the outer deep is the whale, which appears on the arms of Whalley Abbey, that once great establishment on the banks of the Calder, Lancashire ; gules, three whales hauriant, or, in each mouth a crosier of the last.

It is not only the whale which is in the habit of swallowing things. The town of King's Lynn bears : azure, three conger eels' heads erased hauriant, or, in the mouth of each a cross-crosslet fitchy, of the last.

Glasgow affords us a fine example of that curiously world-

CITY OF GLASGOW.

wide legend of a fish restoring a long-lost ring. The arms of the city of Glasgow show on a silver field a green oak-tree growing from a green mount. At the base of the stem, but in front of it, is a salmon on its back, shown in its proper colours, and having a gold signet-ring in its mouth. On the top of the tree is a robin redbreast ; on the left of the tree is an ancient silver handbell. The crest is a half-length figure of a bishop, wearing his vestments and mitre. The right hand is raised in the act of benediction, the left hand

holds a crosier over his shoulder, all being painted in their
natural colours. The supporters are two salmon, each holding
in its mouth a gold-signet ring. Some argue that we have
here purely spiritual symbolism—the oak is the tree of life ;
the bird of the Holy Spirit ; the bell of the Church ; the fish
of our Saviour ; and the ring the emblem of the marriage of
the Church to Christ. Others have a more circumstantial
tale to tell. They say the bishop is the good St. Kentigern,
patron of Glasgow, who founded the city in 500 A.D. Kentigern means " Chief Lord " ; this was softened into Mungo,
" Dear Friend," when he became a missionary and performed many miracles. He breathed on a frozen hazel-branch
and kindled it into flames ; he restored life to the dead robin
of the hermit of St. Serf ; brought a handbell from Rome
which wrought wonders ; and by his intervention the lost
ring of the frail queen Rederech, which had been cast into
the Clyde in sign of marital displeasure, was restored by a
salmon, thus bringing about reconciliation.

Now it must be remembered that the story of throwing a
ring into the sea and its subsequent recovery by means of
a fish which had swallowed it, and all the important events
that followed therefrom, is pretty well as old as the hills,
and met with in many unexpected places. Herodotus tells
us the tale of Polycrates. In the Koran there is a story of
how Satan by sundry wiles secured Solomon's signet and by
virtue thereof sat on his throne for forty days, then, getting
tired, how he threw the ring into the sea. It was swallowed
by a fish which was captured by the wandering and disconso-
late Solomon, who, finding the ring in the fish's belly, thereby
was able to regain his kingdom. That is very much the same
story as told to us by the Glasgow shield. Then in Germany
we find a certain von Findelstein, of Bavaria, bearing : gules,
an arm proceeding from the clouds, habited azure, the hand
grasping a fish with a golden ring in its mouth. Hamilton
of Hogg, bears : gules, a salmon's head couped fesswise
with a ring in its mouth, between three cinquefoils, all argent.
Other instances could be cited both at home and abroad.

Many fish are borne for the sake of a punning allusion to

family names. For instance, pike, of old called lucies, are
borne by the Lucies; Heringham has three herrings hauriant;
Heringot, Kent, (*temp*. Henry III,) bore a border of herrings ;
while Heringod, of Icklesham, Sussex, bore : azure, semée
of cross-crosslets, six herrings naiant in pale, or ; and Heringod, of Elmstead, as seen sculptured on a cloister ceiling of
Canterbury Cathedral, bore : azure, three herrings hauriant
between six crosslets fitchy, or.   Troutbeck of Troutbeck,
Westmorland, a family of feudal descent, bore : azure, three
trout fretted, tête à queue, azure (thus forming a ring).
For crest, a head resting on a wreath of trout. In a Roll of
Arms in the Harleian Collection, British Museum, the three
fish of Troutbeck are shown two in saltire, heads abased, the
third hauriant. Both of these compositions are curious.

Sometimes three fish bodies are borne en pairle, with a
single head in the fess
point. Bream are gener-
ally borne semi-hauriant;
that is, naiant in bend.
Thus De Mare, Abbot
of Peterborough, bore :

KINGSTON-ON-THAMES.   YARMOUTH.

azure, three bream bendwise, two and one, or. The Counts
of Bar, intimately connected with our Plantagenets, bore
two barbel hauriant embowed and addorsed in a field
crusily. But by no means all fish are borne for the sake of
the pun. Many are allusive to important water rights. Thus
Kingston-on-Thames now bears : azure, three salmon naiant
in pale, or, in base a Saxon K, of the last, but formerly

bore : azure, three salmon hauriant in fess, argent; thus reminding us that of old the Thames was a great salmon river. Great Yarmouth formerly bore : azure, three herrings naiant, in pale argent. For centuries past this coat has been dimidiated with the royal arms of England, the lion coat appearing on the dexter side. The result is that we have a shield per pale gules and azure charged with three half lions gold, with herrings tails, argent. Many other towns, such as Poole and Brighton, bear dolphins on their shields.

The arms of Iceland are a golden stockfish (a codfish spread open, deprived of its head and dried) on a blue shield. In Germany we find skeletons of fish emblazoned. Eels are also common charges. In Spain, as we shall see, they were sometimes shown in cauldrons. Crabs and crayfish are shown, and so are many shell-fish. The most celebrated of these are the escallop shells, usually associated with St. James of Compostella and pilgrimage, hence with Crusading, travel beyond the seas, and later with commerce. Alstanton bears : azure, three sea-urchins, needles erect, argent.

Coming to another branch of natural history we find many snakes and serpents. When erect and wavy they are said to be " ondoyant in pale " ; when wriggling across the shield they are " gliding." They are often borne " nowed " and are even found knotted round a human throat. Among the celebrated heraldic snakes is that of Milan, ondoyant in pale and vorant a child, carnation, on a field or. It is supposed to record the prowess of the first Duke of Milan in slaying a monster which levied a tribute of human sacrifices on the Milanese. But the snake is not always an exemplification of evil, though we do see it on heraldic shields representing Satan in the Garden of Eden. It was, however, also one of the creatures sacred to the sun, as in Egypt and India, and stood as a symbol of sun and sun gods ; for instance, Apollo, father of medicine and music. Snakes therefore, are emblems of wisdom and are to be seen wreathed about hand mirrors (the mirror is a sun symbol), about the caduceus and distilling into cups. In this light they are connected both with justice and medicine ; this doubtless also accounts for the Wise bearing: sable, three chevrons between as many adders argent. Others, like the asps of the Aspe family, and the vert, three asps in pale or, of Aspendall, are obviously of punning intent. Ednowain ap Bradwen, Merionethshire, bore : gules, three snakes nowed in triangle argent.

Crocodiles are comparatively modern. A good example is the supporter granted to Speke of Nile exploration fame.

Insects are also seen. These include scorpions, ants, butterflies, bees and grasshoppers. Bees are very ancient emblems, favourites as badges with royal personages as exemplifying an industrious community clustering round their sovereign. They were used by the Romans and by the French kings, but more notably by Napoleon I and his nephew. Bees also represent commerce. Probably the same root notion of association in industry caused the ant and ermite to make their appearance in heraldry. Certainly that appears to be the reason for their presence on the shield of the Benedictine Abbey of Pershore : sable, on a chevron between three ant-hills or, each charged with four ants proper, as many holly-leaves azure. The grasshopper appears in connection with knightly heraldry, and also with the symbols of commerce. A notable example in the latter sense is the golden grasshopper of Sir Thomas Gresham, Lord Mayor of London, Merchant Venturer and Grocer, in the crowded days of Queen Elizabeth.

CHAPTER VII

FABULOUS CREATURES

THERE are many fabulous creatures used in heraldry, a number originating in the dateless symbolism of our remote ancestors, others introduced through the fantasy of romance-loving man, and yet more owing to the freaks of heralds and herald painters. In the main, however, fabulous monsters, especially the humanised beasts, belong to an early stage of mental development, a stage when man looked upon himself as part of natural surroundings, subject to mysterious outside forces but dimly recognised. To him animals and trees were dwellings of kin souls. Hence the worship of animals as manifestations of superhuman forces, as in the ferocious lion, the cunning tiger, the powerful whirl-wind dashing bull. Hence the picturing of the winged, human-headed bulls of Nineveh, the harpies, human-headed lions, the mermen and mermaids. Then came the bird-, beast-, and reptile-headed men and women, which, through totemism or other form of ritual, linked the whole animated world together, as we see in the long gallery of Egyptian deities. So men were shown springing out of the animals, as in the centaur ; then men stood on them ; and finally seated themselves on thrones representing animals, as with the peacock throne of Persia, dwindling down into our own lion-armed crowning chair. As I have pointed out elsewhere : " The science of paleontology has justified many of the queerest monster creations of early artists. There is the grebe-like *hesperonis regalis* of the Rockies, 6 feet high, with long jaws full of teeth ; other birds with prolonged vertebræ, suggestive of snake-like tails, and paws of reptiles with strong claws." (" Armorial Insignia of the Princes of Wales.")

GRIFFIN RAMPANT.   STUCCO TOURNEY SHIELD.

Foremost among those monsters which particularly interest us are the dragons, a formidable army, springing from the mysterious East, the Nilithic swamps and the morasses of Northern Europe as well as of our own islands. For there are many types. Judaic dragons were amphibious, created with the fishes (Genesis 1) ; in Isaiah we are told of " the dragon that lieth in the sea " ; and in Ezekiel of the " great dragon that lieth in the midst of the rivers," which was Tiamat, the prodigiously huge four-legged, scaly-bodied she-dragon of Chaldea and Babylon, whom Bel, god of Nippon,

CITY OF LONDON.   DRAGON
SUPPORTERS.

lord of the Underworld, overcame, and whom Marduk, the winged solar-god slew, splitting her in half to make the sky and the earth.

In the Far East the dragon is usually serpentine in form, with four legs, rugged head with spiked ears and is an aerial, but wingless brute. The Chinese Imperial dragon is golden, but silver or white on the standard, with blue scales, has five claws and is represented as attacking the sun, having long feelers projecting from its jaws circling round the golden or scarlet disc. As a symbol of delegated power appertaining to high officials, its colour and number of talons varied according to rank. The Japanese dragon rises from the

5

sea and has only three claws to each of its feet. In the Near East the dragon is an aerial-amphibian, with long reptilian, scaly body, four short paws with formidable talons and saurian head with spiked ears, fangs and forked tongue, bat-like wings, and generally belches forth fire. It is this type that we see in Christian iconography trodden under foot by the Archangel Michael, St. George or other hero, and is represented in the badge of the Knights of the Garter. Something similar, though often having only two legs, was the common dragon of the Norsemen and Celtic people. It may be seen in the Bayeux tapestry, both among the Norman knights and Harold's followers. But there were dragons here before the Normans or even the Saxons came, for Geoffrey of Monmouth in his " Chronicle " tells us of the British Uther seeing a dragon-shaped comet in the sky, adopted a golden dragon as his war standard, and henceforth was known as Uther Pendragon. This legendary Pendragon was sire to the shadowy King Arthur. But Pendragon appears to have been a warrior title, for the Saxon chronicles tell us of Cedric's victory over Naud and his Pendragon, at a place which some have identified as Dragon's Hill, Berkshire.

After the Conquest the dragon was well to the fore. Richard I had a dragon standard when he went Crusading, and Henry III had a golden dragon, with wagging tongue and eyes of sapphire, borne before him at Westminster, and possibly at the disastrous battle of Lewes. Edward I marched into Wales under a golden dragon standard, and Edward III had it at Crecy. Edward IV had as a badge a black dragon segreant, with gold claws, which he had adopted when he became Earl of Ulster, deriving it through the Mortimers from the de Burghs, the first Earls of Ulster. Then came the Tudor rulers from Henry VII to Elizabeth, with their ruddy-gold, or gold and red squat dragons. It must be said that the Welsh dragon of war was red, but the righteous dragon was of ruddy gold. In Tudor days the under part was red, the upper gold.

At a fairly early date the heraldic dragon as depicted on coat armour was of a lionine type, having squat scaly body, long legs with claws, barbed saurian tail, rugged head with horny projections, barbed tongue, and great bat wings. It

DRAGON.   GRIFFIN.
UNICORN.   HARPY.

is borne " volant," " segreant " (rampant), as in the Tudor and the City of London supporters, passant, as in the Welsh badge, and is used as a charge, a crest or badge and for supporters. The serpentine form as a crest is shown on the helm of Roger, Earl of Winchester (1195-1265) (page 217). A dragon with a human head is blazoned as "monstreu." Dragons' heads and wings are met as charges and as crests. Field-Marshal Lord Beresford, for his victory at Albuera in 1811, received for crest : out of a mural crown, a dragon's head, pierced by a lance, which it holds between its teeth ; typifying the tenacious bravery of both vanquished and victors.

Winged serpents are also borne in heraldry, and apparently owe their parentage to the symbolism of ancient Egypt, where we find two opposing armies of winged ophidians, the evil ones warring against Osiris (the sun god) during his nightly passage through the Underworld, and the beneficent guardians of the noon-day sun, frequently seen wreathed about the solar disc. Both types may be represented in intricate knots (like the attenuated ribbon dragon with bird's neck and beak of the Celts), knots of all kinds standing for mystic "words of power." These are the "amphiptere" of French blazonry.

Wyverns, so constantly blazoned, are really the early type of serpentine dragon, having only two legs and a long tail, generally "nowed." It is the type of dragon still used in Continental heraldry.

The hydra, the many-headed serpent of classic legend, whom Hercules slew, is occasionally borne. A notable example is afforded by the arms granted to Ossip Ivanovich, who saved the life of the Emperor Alexander II in 1865. He bore : or, issuant from the sinister flank an arm proper, vested azure, the hand seizing a hydra sable, winged gules ; on a chief of the third a ship fully rigged bearing the Imperial standard, all proper.

Local monsters are to be seen in the shields of some towns and territorial magnates, as in the case of Tarascon, with its fierce tarask, a kind of dragon-basilisk.

Griffins, or gryphons, were known both to the Greeks and the Romans, as their sculptures and coins testify. No doubt they came from the East, perhaps by way of Egypt. They have the forequarters of dragons, the hindquarters of lions, eagles' heads with prominent pointed ears, and small bat wings. These ears are of great importance in distinguishing

GRECIAN GRIFFIN.

the griffin, for it is said to have been one of the fiercest, most active, and quickest of animals. They are emblems of vigilance, so the pointed eared head as crest or charge is a favourite. Gerard Leigh, a herald of the time of Queen Elizabeth, speaking of griffins, in a manner clearly showing he believed that they had a real existence, says, " I think they are of great hugeness, for I have a claw of one of their paws which should show them to be as big as two lions." Lady Mary Wortley Montagu in one of her chatty letters, dated from Ratisbon (in 1716), mentions having been shown in a Roman Catholic church a huge claw set in gold, which

HAWK-HEADED HORUS.

was said to be a griffin's claw. " I could not," says Lady Mary, " forbear asking the reverend priest that showed it, whether the griffin was a saint ? The question almost put him beside his gravity, but he answered they only kept it as a curiosity."

A cockatrice is a wyvern with a cock's head, but barbed tongue.

A harpy has the head and bust of a woman and the body of an eagle, and like so many other of these monsters may be traced through classical art to Eastern imagery.

Sphinxes, with their lionine bodies and women's busts and heads, belong to the mysticism of Egypt, and, though known to the Romans, only appear to have entered the realms of heraldry towards the end of the eighteenth century, when the land of the Nile began to be a field for European enterprise. It is one of the war badges of several of our regiments. Sir John Moore, the hero of Corunna, in honour of his earlier services in Egypt, bore : argent, on a fess engrailed azure, three mullets of the field, in chief a sphinx proper, all within a border engrailed.

Unicorns also reached the Greeks and Romans from the East, for they thought the beasts were to be found in India, though some kinds of African quadrupeds are far more likely to have given the idea. Indeed, a perfect representation of the unicorn is to be seen on a Roman-Egyptian papyrus in our national collection at the British Museum. It is there shown seated in a chair playing a losing game of draughts with a smirking lion. Unicorns of this description are also to be found in far older hieroglyphic inscriptions in the land of Osiris. It is amusing to find this antagonism between the two beasts shown in this way, for the legend of their enmity is one of the firm beliefs of old-time writers. This was unfortunate, for while the lion was regarded as the symbol of martial valour, the unicorn stood for purity, the protector of virtue. Its horn was regarded as a sovereign cure for many dire diseases, a grand antidote against all poisons. Many royal and other collections in mediæval days and somewhat later contained fragments of unicorn horns. In an inventory of royal jewels made for Queen Elizabeth we find mentioned, " Imprimis, a piece of unicorn's horn," and some time later a German traveller, one Hentzner, saw at Windsor Castle " a horn of about eight spans and a half in length, valued at about £10,000." These and other such horns are well authenticated, and presumably were the teeth of narwhals. The heraldic unicorn has the body of a horse, the legs of a stag, the tail of a lion, a fine mane, and a single horn springing from its forehead. It is almost invariably white or silver, but it is usually armed and unguled of gold. Such is the famous unicorn supporter of the royal arms of the United Kingdom, brought to us from Scotland by James I. This unicorn is gorged with a royal crown, with a chain attached and reflexed over its back. The unicorn is used as a charge, a crest and a supporter. Both the Chinese and the Japanese have a unicorn, which has the body and hoofs of a deer, the tail of an ox, and a horn on its forehead. So it is not unlike our own, only rather heavier in build. Curiously enough its companion is also a lion, the so-called " dog of Buddha," which has tufts of curling hair round the neck and on the limbs. This rather assimilates it to the Assyrian lion, with its elaborately plaited mane and solemn mien, so different to attitude and expression as characteristic of our own " leopards."

The heraldic antelope must be mentioned here, for it is like nothing seen in nature, with its body of a stag, but fantastic head, a great horn growing upon the tip of its nose, and its grotesque tufts of hair down its neck, back, on its chest, thighs and tip of its tail. There is, however, a later antelope, with two horns, and altogether more natural, introduced by modern African adventurers of all sorts.

Henry Fitzroy, Duke of Richmond, natural son of Henry VIII, derived the yale as one of his supporters from his mother. It is described as " a yale argent bezanty, horned, hoofed and gorged with a crown and chained or," and is an heraldic antelope with the horns of a ram and the tail of a dog.

Salamanders are short-tailed, horny skinned lizards, having four fairly long legs, and are usually shown gambolling amidst flames and breathing fire. Legend said that the salamander was of so cold a nature that it could extinguish flames, and

appears in earlier symbolism to have been adopted as an
emblem of religious ardour and of faith overcoming trials ;
later as representing perseverance overcoming worldly troubles
of all kinds.   It is probably from a mixture of the two ideas
that the salamander was adopted as the badge of Comtes
d'Angoulême, from whom it descended to Francis I, who has
left splendid examples of his royally crowned cognisance,
carved, painted and traced in needlework at the Château de

IRONMONGERS' COMPANY, LONDON.   SALAMANDER CREST
AND SUPPORTERS.

Blois.   It was under one of these that the following lines
were inscribed :

"Ursus atrox, Aquilæque leves, et Tortilis anguis
    Cesserunt flammæ cain Salamander tuæ."

This, of course, refers to the French king's victories over the
Swiss, Germans and Milanese, who are represented by their
national emblems of the bear, the eagle and the serpent.   As
in the case of the badge of François, salamanders may be
blazoned gorged with a crown or coronet, with chain attached,
and reflexed over the back.

Another creature associated with flames is the phœnix,

SALAMANDER AMIDST FLAMES.   BADGE OF FRANCIS I.

or mystic golden sun eagle. It was known to and honoured by the Egyptians as a religious emblem representing the continuity of life. They held that when the phœnix grew old it flew into the sun or into a fire, immolating itself. A worm sprang out of its ashes, and out of the worm was hatched a full-fledged young phœnix. This parable of the efficacy of self-sacrifice was seized upon by the early Christians, and the phœnix rising from the flames may be found in the Catacombs of Rome, representing belief in the doctrine of resurrection. It was in this sense that it was welcomed in armoury, where it is represented as an eagle displayed rising from flames, the head turned skywards. The usual tinctures for the eagle are sable or gold. In China and Japan the phœnix is the badge of the Empresses.

A pegasus is a winged horse, generally represented as " volant " and " animé " (with an eye of a different tincture to the body itself). It is the winged steed of Apollo, so largely connected with intellectual arts. Thus Rusticuli, of Italy, bear : or, on a mount of Parnassus vert, with springs of water, azure, a pegasus of the third. Our Michael Drayton had the better shield : azure, gutty d'argent, a pegasus of the second. The pegasus borne as the arms of the Inner Temple is said to be a mere imposition. One of the badges of the Knights Templar was a horse on which two knights were mounted, in allusion to their vow of poverty. Probably unwilling to take such a vow the lawyers transformed the two poor warriors into two wings. Sir John Jervis (Lord St. Vincent), for his victory off Cape St. Vincent, was assigned the following crest when raised to the peerage : a pegasus springing from a naval crown, its wings charged with a fleur-de-lis.

Centaurs belong to classic legend, wherein they found their way from the dark regions beyond the Caucasus, those lands where man seemed to form one with his steed. The centaur has a horse's body, but from the shoulders up the bust, arms and head of a man. It was an emblem of courage, tempered with wisdom. When a centaur bears bows and arrows it is blazoned as a " sagitarius," and appears quite early as one

of the signs of the zodiac. A "sagitarius" was possibly
adopted as a badge by our King Stephen.

The manticora and the chimera both belong to this class.
A manticora, also known as a lampago, or a man tiger, has
the body of an heraldic tiger with the head of an old man
adorned with long spiral horns. A manticora of purple was
the badge of Lord Fitzwalter (*temp*. Henry VII or earlier).
Probably his son, described as "Master Ratleefe" (Ratcliffe)
in the "Book of Standards" of the Heralds' College, had
one not only with human head, but feet as well, crowned with
a cap of dignity, with a chain of gold round its neck and a
sun pendent therefrom beneath a padlock. A chimera has
the body of a goat, the face of a man, mane and legs of a
lion, and tail of a dragon. Luckily she is only encountered
as a crest.

Almost all animals have been represented at one time or
another in heraldry with fishes' tails, when they are said
to be "marined." First among these is man, together with
his helpmate. Mermen or tritons are seen represented in
the earliest Greek and Roman sculptures. They have the
upper part of the body human, ending either in a single fish
tail, or each leg from the thigh down is separately "marined."
They usually carry tridents and conch-shell trumpets, and
may be wreathed about the head with seaweed. River
tritons usually carry vases and have wreaths of bulrushes.
They are among the symbols of sea power, and are often
associated with the arms of seaports and sailors. An interesting example of how this could come about, although it is
extremely bad heraldry, is afforded by the insignia of Sir
Isaac Heard, Garter-King-at-Arms, who flourished at the
end of the eighteenth century, and who had been a sailor
in his early manhood. He bore : argent, a triton proper,
crowned or, a trident in his dexter hand, his sinister hand
grasping the mast of a ship issuing from the sea in base ;
on a chief azure, the arctic star of the first, between two water
bowgets of the second. The elucidation of this complicated
composition is that Heard was saved from drowning after
shipwreck.

Mermaids, the melosines of the French, are much more interesting. Appropriately enough the goddesses of both Phœnicia and Babylonia were mermaids. The heraldic mermaids have long hair, partly covering the shoulders and breasts, and may have single or double tails. They usually

BRISTOL MERCHANT ADVENTURERS. SUPPORTERS, A MERMAID AND A WINGED SATYR. BARRY WAVY OF S ARGENT AND AZURE, ON A BEND OR A DRAGON PASSANT IN BEND VERT, ON A CHIEF GULES, A LION PASSANT GUARDANT GOLD BETWEEN TWO BEZANTS.

carry a comb in one hand and a mirror in the other, but a German crowned example is armless, with two fish wings, each charged with three barbels embowed. A mermaid holding a dagger is the crest of Harry, co. Cornwall. This forms a very favourite composition, both as a charge and as a crest, and was used to represent sea-service, exploration and over-seas commerce.

Some other of the marined animals deserve special attention.

Sea-horses in the earliest heraldic examples closely resemble the queer fish known by that name (the *hippocampus*), but classic art had furnished quite another type, the forequarters of a horse, with mane and hoofs, and the hindquarters replaced by a fish's tail. Neptune and Boreas were often shown riding these steeds over crested waves. The common type of heraldic charge shows a horse with webbed feet, a scalloped fin down its back and a fish's tail.

Sea-lions, lions with fishes' tails, may often have been produced by heraldic manipulation of two different coats, as was shown in the preceding chapter when describing the dimidiated shield of Yarmouth. The dimidiated shield of Hastings in the same way gives us a lion-ship, for the arms of Hastings are azure, an ancient galley between two lions passant guardant in pale, or; which was dimidiated with England, so that the charge is converted into a half-lion with a ship for hindquarters. But the sea-lion was known to the ancients. With us it is one of the symbols of sea dominion and has been largely employed as a crest or supporter, to commemorate naval victories. For instance, the Earls of Thanet and Viscounts Falmouth bore a sea-horse as crest and had two sea-lions, argent, gutty de sang, as supporters, these having been granted to their ancestor, Admiral Boscawen. Viscount Bridport for his services as second admiral in command on June 1, 1794, was granted a sea-lion and an archer as his supporters.

Sea-dogs are male otters, which, as a matter of fact, often go out considerable distances in the sea. They, however, are depicted with webbed feet, fins down their backs and scaly bodies. They are seen on the arms of Fenner, Sussex: argent, a chevron engrailed gules, between three marine wolves or sea-dogs, sable, finned and dented of the second. Sea otters are the supporters of Lord Stourton.

A marine cock is borne by Geyss of Bavaria, and a sea-horse by Gundriphen of Suabia. Marined griffins and unicorns are also seen in German heraldry. Other marined animals are the sea-stag and the capricorn, the half-goat, half-fish zodiacal sign.

The vertical union of two animals, as the left-hand side of an eagle joined to the right hand half of a lion, occasionally seen on the Continent, is due to dimidiation. I know of no example of such mechanical hybridisation in our own heraldry.

By way of appropriate tail-piece it may be mentioned Lord Stawell has a satyr as one of his supporters, and that Satan, with horns, a cloven foot and barbed tail complete, sometimes occurs in Continental heraldry, which is not so astonishing when we remember that in France we find the patronymics Le Diable softened into Le Maudit, Le Mallin, and Le Mauvais, and in Germany Teufel into Manteufel.

DRAGON ON SHIELD,
BAYEUX TAPESTRY.

CHAPTER VIII

THE HUMAN FORM AND ITS PARTS

MAN appeared rather late in recognised heraldry, and then seemingly by accident. Certainly the knights of the eleventh and twelfth centuries did not place human figures on their shields or on their surcoats. But such figures, generally of a religious description, were occasionally represented on standards, and even more frequently effigies of the owners, or of some allegorical import, were seen on seals, those alike of knights, ecclesiastics, ladies of high estate and corporations. There are a good many indications that seals, both of ecclesiastics and corporate bodies (quite commonly pictorially symbolical), were given an heraldic character by placing the compositions on shields. Many episcopal arms—those of the sees of Chichester and Waterford are good examples—and of towns, such as Bristol, Scarborough, Huntingdon (the latter with a pictorial design of a tree and bird, a huntsman blowing on a horn and two dogs coursing a stag), provide other instances. The Scarborough arms as registered at the College of Arms are without tinctures, but may be described thus : in base a wavy sea, thereon to dexter an ancient ship of one mast with rigging and castellated top, in prow and stern the heads of two men affronté, on sinister side an old castle, a tower thereon, with a Moor's head appearing over the battlements ; in honour point, between castle and ship,

SCARBOROUGH CORPORA-
TION SEAL.

a wavy star of eight points. Lichfield's bearings are
even more extraordinary : on a shield is a landscape with
several trees on a hill to the dexter, a view of the Cathedral
on the sinister, and in base the bodies, heads and limbs
of three naked men scattered over the field together with
crowns, swords and banners. It was in this way that angels,
saints, pilgrims, knightly patrons or mere civic officers (like
that forest warden of Huntingdon), came to be added to
the treasury of available charges. When the step was once
taken, precedents enough could be found, for classic lore told
us of the horrific head of Medusa on Achilles's shield, which
he derived from the target of Pallas Athene (a reminiscence
of the barbaric habit of warriors adorning themselves with
the scalps of their victims).

From the ecclesiastical group the following among the
most notable may be given. On the blue shield of the see
of Chichester, Christ sits on a golden throne, with sword
issuant from mouth, the right hand lifted in benediction. On
the blue shield of the see of Waterford is a bishop in full
canonicals holding a large crucifix in front of him. Moelor
Crwm, of Wales, bore : argent on a chevron sable three angels
kneeling, their hands on their breasts, wings displayed or.
Beringer bore (*circa* 1413) : gules, an angel erect, hands conjoined on breast, wings displayed. Other angels appear, but
they are more frequently seen as crests or supporters. The
angel in elaborate armorial tabards, supporting the lilied
shield of the French kings, is well known. We also have
cherubs as charges, which could scarcely have been designed
for the old schoolmasters, unless in a spirit of imposing abnega-
tion. But we find Saint bearing three cherubs with differently
coloured wings. By the way, the Gothic painter-decorators
were quite fond of giving their angels (many of them forming
corbels supporting armorial shields) red, blue, green, yellow
and even party coloured wings, so that they have a gaudy
parrot appearance. Saints themselves are often found—on
shields. We have seen St. Mungo in connection with the arms
of Glasgow. The insignia for the episcopal district of the Isles
is : azure, on waves of the sea in base, St. Columba kneeling

in a coracle, holding a dove, all proper, looking at a blazing
star, or. For the see of Aberdeen we have : azure, in the
porch of a church, St. Nicolas in pontificals, his right hand
blessing three children in a cauldron, holding in his sinister
hand a crosier, all proper. This bears allusion to the good
saint's restoring life to the children boiled by Myra. Halifax
bears the holy face of St. John the Baptist, thus : chequy
or and azure, the head of St. John affronté, distilling three
goutes of sang from neck, a nimbus about the head, or, in
chief the word " Haley," in base the word " Fax," in Saxon
letters countercharged of the field. The parish church was
dedicated to St. John. In France St. Denis appears in coat
armour.

Our first parents have not been forgotten. Adamoli, of
Lombardy, bears : azure the Tree of Life, entwined with the
Serpent and accosted by Adam and Eve, all proper (but
not from the prude's point of view, for the man and the
woman appear in a state of innocence). Sampson, of
Verona, bore : gules, on a terrace, vert, Sampson (gilded,
but *sans culottes* or clothes of any kind) bestriding a
golden lion and tearing his jaws apart. Hercules is seen on
Continental coats fighting with a lion, with a hydra, and
rending a tree. Apollo, as god of the sun, of music and
medicine, is frequently borne. On the arms of the Apothe-
caries' Company, London, he is blazoned as a Roman knight,
bestriding a dragon, and wielding a bow and arrow.
Atlas appears bearing the world on his back, Vulcan armed
with his hammer, Mars in war panoply and Neptune with
his trident and net. Bacchus may bear his grape-twined
thyrsus ; but the German coat of Hopfer bears, punningly :
or, the infant Bacchus, dancing, wreathed about his loins
and head with hops, with a bunch of hops in his hand. Which
calls to mind the quaint blazonry of the city of Dantzic :
or, in a field gules two couples (*chacun sa chacune*, as we might
say), dancing, proper ; in chief an eagle displayed, in base
a cross, both sable. Sobieski's personal coat was : or, a
queen, hair dishevelled or, habited gules, seated on a bear
passant, sable, her arms extended in cross. Rather easier

ITALIAN PANEL, SIXTEENTH CENTURY.

to read is the rebus of Richard Barnes, Bishop of Carlisle, 1570 : azure, on a bend argent between two stars or, a bear passant guardant powdered with golden stars, ready to devour a naked boy ; on a chief silver three roses gules radiant gold. Another version shows the naked boy full faced and grasping in his hands the tongue of a bear. How a youngster may be made to point a moral was shown by an early Oswald, who bore : azure, a naked boy pointing to a star in the dexter chief. A later worldly Oswald altered this to : azure, a savage wreathed about the loins with bay-leaves, having a sheath of arrows hanging by his side, bearing a bow in his sinister hand, and pointing with the dexter to a coronet placed in the dexter chief. Queen Mary bore as one of her badges a figure of winged Time drawing Truth from a well, with the motto " Veritas temperis filia." Fortune (like Truth) appears as a nude female, erect on a wheel or on a globe. Crehall has : argent, two bars azure, over all on dexter side a naked man proper, hands over head holding a pellet, on sinister an oak-tree eradicated vert ; Drummond : or, three bars undy gules, over all a naked man naiant in pale, grasping in dexter hand a sword, his sinister hand and both feet in action, proper. But how he came to swim in that sea of blood we know not.

A naked man of very doubtful antecedents appears on the sable shield of the Scottish Dalzells. Originally he was shown as standing full face, with arms extended in the form of the cross. Then he was lifted aloft and dangled, still *sans sark*, from a gallow tree. Since then he has been unhooked and now appears, still full faced and unashamed, but with his arms close to his thighs, as though at attention. He is of carnation or " proper." To this shield Lord Carnwath has added as supporters two armed men in ancient costume. The legend runs that the original Dalzell recovered from the gallows for King Kenneth II the corpse of a kinsman who had been hung (and no doubt deservedly so) in a border raid. But the whole affair is suspicious.

Tragedies of one kind or another, however, are not uncommon on armorial shields. We have already seen the

6

Milanese serpent devouring a boy. Grimsditch, of Chester (*temp*. Henry III), bore a griffin seizing a man in complete armour lying on his back; Warnchampe : vert, a wyvern passant volant argent, swallowing a child carnation. Barragan, of Navarre, bore : or, a naked corpse, proper, at foot of a tree, vert, a raven at head and one at feet, sable. Davies, a Welshman, bore : sable, a goat argent, attired or, standing on a child, proper, swaddled gules, and feeding from a tree vert.

Warriors are borne in many forms. If fully accounted in armour, he is blazoned a " chevalier," and may be borne on foot or mounted. Admiral Kempenfelt bore a chevalier with a sword above the head, and Horman bore a demi-man in armour. Blacker bore : argent, gutty de sang, a Danish warrior armed with battle-axe and sword in his hands all proper. They are more commonly seen as supporters, as in the case of Lord Carnwath with his primitive kilted Lowlanders, the Earl of Leven with his men-at-arms of Charles I's day, and many others, coming down to those with soldiers of modern times. Wood bore : azure, three wild men of the woods proper, holding in their dexter hands clubs argent, and in their sinister hands silver escutcheons, each charged with a cross gules. Chisholm, of Inverness-shire, who trace their ancestry from Harold, Thane of Caithness, Orkney and Shetland in the twelfth century, bear : azure, a boar's head erased, argent ; and for supporters two naked wild men, wreathed about their loins, carrying clubs, to represent the war-like clansmen. But for this branch of the subject readers should turn to Chapter XXII.

Comares, of Spain, bears : argent, a Moorish king passant, habited azure, with collar round his neck and chain attached, or ; evidently a prisoner. More peaceful are the arms of Lylde, otherwise Thomas de Insula, Bishop of Ely, 1341-61: gules, on three bezants the Kings of Cologne (the Magi of the Nativity). Middleton, of Belsay Castle, Northamptonshire, whose ancestor, (*temp*. Edward III), acquired valuable estates by marriage, a fact recorded by the naked wild men, wreathed about the loins and head, holding a fructed oak-tree in his hand. Similar in spirit is the demi-huntsman winding a horn, the crest of Clerk of Perth. In the same class of landed interests is the German coat of Roten : azure, a woman in old national costume carrying a fish in each hand. In some instances the maiden's arms are replaced by fish, a quaint Teutonic reversion to the old Greek metamorphised girls.

We have seen that a demi-man may be borne. This is natural as a crest, but when it occurs as a charge on a shield it is no doubt usually the result of some form of dimidiation, or the introduction of a crest or badge. But it is quite possible that in some cases the symbolism may have been intentional, for under feudal tenure many subtenants held land subject to the provision in time of war of half an armed man. That is, he had to join with some other tenant in providing a man-at-arms.

When we come to heads (which, together with other parts of the body, were depicted on shields much earlier than man as a whole), whether borne " coupecd " (cut off smoothly at the neck) or " eradicated " (torn off with a jagged edge) we are undoubtedly in a region of war badges, for they are associated with the Medusa mask (that face distorted by fury, the tresses of hair replaced by curled and hissing snakes attached to the scalp). The long contest during the middle ages between Christendom and Mohammedanism in Europe, Africa and the Near East was largely responsible for the adoption of heads of Saracens, Moors and Turks as war badges among the Hungarians, Italians and Spaniards, these gradually finding their way into the universals of heraldry. The Saracen's head is generally that of a black, with a wreath of twisted linen across his forehead. Such a head appears in the arms of Gladstone, the forehead wreathed with green leaves. Sardinia bears : argent, a cross gules, between four Moors' heads couped, sable, banded (that is, wreathed with the linen twist) of the first. This tells of the constant invasion of that island by followers of the Prophet. Corsica was also subject to these incursions, and its old arms were : argent, a Saracen's head, sable, banded across the eyes of the first ; but when

Paoli had almost won freedom for his native isle, he lifted the bandage from the eyes to the forehead. It is Corsica's Saracen's head which is seen on the arms of the Earls of Minto, as a memento of Sir Gilbert Elliot's unfortunate governorship of that island. While Newton bore : sable, a Saracen's head couped at neck, argent, with three lions' jambs in dexter, sinister and base points or ; Best had : gules a Saracen's head couped at neck proper, navally crowned or, between eight lions' jambs, chevronwise in pairs inwards gold. These look like British sailors' victories over Corsairs. But it is necessary to be cautious in this matter for the families of both Mores and Moores bear Moors' heads ; so did the Malatestas and the Testis of Italy. Lloyd of Plymog bore : gules, a chevron ermine, between three heads couped at neck, bearded and crined sable. These arms, tradition asserts, were given to Edryfed Vysham ap Kendrig, Lord of Bryffenigh, Denily, by the Prince of North Wales (*temp*. John), for his victory over the English under the Earl of Chester, when he slew three of the chief leaders. Through marriage and descent these three English heads have been carried on to many a respectable family shield. Rochead, a Scot, with his argent, a savage's head couped, distilling blood proper, between three black combs, is somewhat enigmatical, but it looks like the gratification of an itch for a bad joke.

Women's heads, with long flowing hair, occur. One of the oldest and most important of the City Guilds, the Mercers' Company, bears : azure, within an orle of clouds, argent, the head of a virgin, vested argent, crowned with a celestial crown or, and wreathed about the temples gules. This represents the Virgin Mary, patron of the Guild and the whole corporate body of Mercers. Reading bears : azure, the head of a virgin ducally crowned, between four virgins' heads (this forming a saltire) all proper, crined, or. [Reading was noted for its religious foundations, and probably the heads represent the Virgin Mary and four local martyrs, saintly patrons of conventual establishments. It is amusing to find that when William Camden made a re-grant of these arms in the days of Queen Elizabeth, he added to the

blazoning the letters " R " and " E," and in the spirit of
this rather ill-placed homage, the central head has sometimes
been regally crowned.] Queen Catherine Parr's badge was a
dainty conception : a maiden's head issuing from a Tudor
rose.   The Herberts of Pembrokeshire have as a crest a
Moorish girl's head, couped at the shoulders, hair dishevelled,
and rings in her ears.   Vaughan, Breconshire, bears : azure,
three boys' heads couped argent, having snakes knotted
round their necks; and one of the early Lords Willoughby
had a full-faced Moor's head, without neck, the tongue
hanging out, as his badge.   Janer, of Spain, placed the head
of Janue on his shield.   Jay bore: argent, three Midas's heads
(with donkey's ears) sable ; while the French Santeuils chose
the head of Argus, which was represented as a human head
covered from scalp to bust with wide-open eyes, perhaps a
tithe of that hundred which phonetics demanded.   The
ermine, three princes' heads couped at breast, crowned and
mantled proper, of Enfant and Fauntleroy ; the gules, three
boys' heads couped argent, crined or, of Infant ; and the
gules, three maidens' heads argent, crined or, of Madeston
are quite understandable.   Henry Man, Bishop of Sodor and
Man, 1546–56, adopted an extraordinary design for his
shield : azure, a masculyn (a large mascle), and within it
five youths' heads couped argent, crined or.   Heads are
also borne on swords and lances, and the crest of Thomas de
Barwe (Barrow), Lord of the Manor of Newington Barrow
(Highbury), shows an eagle pecking at the eyes of a head.
This brings us to skulls, shown alone or as the famous " death's
head and cross-bones " (thigh-bones borne in saltire), which
appeared on the *Jolly Roger* or pirate's flag, and also as the
regimental badge of the 17th Lancers.   Bolters bore : argent,
on a chevron gules, three human skulls silver ; and Damboys :
paly of six or and gules a jaw-bone in pale, azure.

Even skeletons are not unknown ; de la Sabloniere, of
Holland, bore : argent, two skeletons, sable, holding between
them a sieve, argent.   Evidently they were supposed to be
sanding, in punning allusion to the bearers.   In France,
Italy and Portugal the families of Costa, Costanza, Coste and

others having similar names placed ribs on their shields, just as our Baines have crossed thigh and shin bones.

Eyes are, of course, among primitive symbols. In Christian iconography when placed within a triangle or a triquestra an eye represented the Deity, and these devices are occasionally found in connection with ecclesiastical armoury. But human eyes are more common. They are sometimes shown weeping, as in the case of the French family of Denis.

Human hearts, of the purely conventional shape, are favourite charges. They are shown with flames springing from the artery and vein ; pierced by one, two or three arrows, by nails, by swords ; or borne on the points of swords or lances. While some are given wings which may silently recall earthly or other wordly desires, others on the contrary are placed within fetterlocks. One of the most famous of the heraldic hearts is that appearing on the coat of the Douglas family. These arms originally were : argent, on a chief azure, three mullets of the field ; but to this, about 1333, William, Lord Douglas, added a red heart, placing it on the silver field ; about fifty years later a golden crown was placed on the heart. Now this augmentation was to commemorate the entrusting by Robert Bruce to Sir James Douglas the duty of carrying his heart to be buried in the Holy Land. When the king was dead, Sir James set out with his precious burden, but fell fighting against the Moors in Spain, in 1330. Jacques Cœur, the generous French merchant and financial adviser to the king, who flourished about the middle of the fifteenth century, bore these canting arms : azure, on a fess or, between three hearts, or, as many escallop shells, gules, with the motto " A cœur vaillant rien d'impossible." The Amants, also of France, had another, more subtle, pictorial pun on their name : azure, a chevron between three hearts inflamed, gules. Cheylau's heart sent forth a pansy, which is delightful, while more politically inclined versions of the same idea are seen in the fleur-de-lis sprouting from hearts. Colleoni, of Italy, bear : per pale argent and gules, three hearts reversed and counterchanged ; that is to say, the hearts are upside down, one silver, the other red and the third half red and half white. But this is a very much softened version of the arms borne by that redoubtable swashbuckling condottiere, Colleoni of Milan, and his immediate descendants, which was a startling example of *armes parlantes*, conceived in a spirit worthy of brave old Cyrano de Bergerac, that pioneer voyager to the land of the Moon.

Hands and arms are borne under many guises. The fist may be closed ; the thumb and two first fingers raised in the attitude of blessing ; or the open palm, styled "appaumé," may be shown. It may be couped at the wrist or erased with jagged edge. The blessing hand is appropriately borne by Benoit : azure, three hands blessing, argent ; and this same hand is also seen as the crest of the Scottish Millars. The red open hand, cut at the wrist, is the "Bloody Hand of Ulster," really the red hand of O'Neil, Earl of Tyrone. The legend attaching to its adoption is that when a fleet of marauding northerners were intent on invading Erin, the original O'Neil severed his hand with his sword and flung it on shore, thus taking possession, *manus militaris*, before any of his companions could do so. It is worth while comparing this with the legend concerning the

CREST OF WINGED HANDS.

two hands in the coat-of-arms of the city of Antwerp ; gules, a castle of four towers, in chief a dexter and sinister hand appaumé, couped at the wrist, all or. It is said that when Julius Cæsar was invading Gaul a kind of peninsula in the Scheldt was fortified like a castle, and therein dwelt a giant who levied toll on all who passed up and down the river, cutting off the right hand of any who tried to evade the tariff, and flinging the severed member into the river. This castle was seized by Salvias Brabo, King of Tangres, and lieutenant of Cæsar, who cut off the tyrant's head and hands, consigning them to a watery grave, an event commemorated by Jef Lombeaux's fine fountain and statue before the Town Hall, and also by the charges on the civic shield. As regards Tyrone's red hand, this became famous or otherwise, when it was adopted as the badge of the new hereditary order of knights, the baronets, an order instituted by James I with a view to raise money to colonise Ulster. Since then all baronets of Ireland and of the United Kingdom have borne on their paternal coats an inescutcheon argent, charged with a hand appaumé, couped at the wrist, gules.

Traditions relating to the symbolism of the hand are numerous. According to Mahomedans the open hand illustrates the five associated points of the true religion : profession of faith, prayer, almsgiving, fasting, and pilgrimage. More generally the five fingers are taken to represent power, knowledge, will, worthiness, duty ; or force, authority, love, obedience : but in all cases the necessity for united effort is enforced. The right hand, open or closed, has always stood for power and authority, for it was the sword and spear wielder, and when placed on a sceptre became a veritable sign manual of the ruler. So sometimes an eye is placed in the palm of an open hand, to show the vigilance of ruling power ; though when associated with the blessing hand it represents the Divine sanction of the act. It is this recognition of the authority of the right hand that led to the policy of severing that member from prisoners, whether of war or criminals. Of course, it is not all hands that have this exalted origin, for there are several coats belonging to the same order as that of Baron Castlemaine, whose family name is Handcock, and who bears : ermine, on a chief, sable, a dexter hand between two cocks argent, armed, crested and jelloped gules. Thus the Tremaynes have three hands ; some branches of the family three bent arms, joined at the shoulders and arranged en pairle, the palms of the hands open. Henry de Malmaine in the days of the Plantagenets bore : or, three sinister hands gules ; and the modern Maynards change the tincture of the field to argent. Hands are shown grasping many things, such as swords, lances, cups and so on. Two hands clasped and winged at the wrists make a charming emblem of ardent friendship.

ARMS OF ANTWERP.

Arms are borne " embowed," or bent, and may be naked, " manched " or " habited." If clothed in armour they are said to be " vambraced." A " cubit arm " is one cut off above the wrist, but below the elbow. Sir John Care, an old-time knight, bore as his badge a dexter arm issuing from the clouds, habited gules, cuffed ermine, holding in the hand blue columbines with green leaves. Sometimes chaplets are held ; but more frequently one sees weapons of war ; and quite as often the hand grasps a snake, a human throat, or that of a beast.

In Continental heraldry we frequently see a dexter and sinister arm issuing from the flanks of the shield, the hands clasped in the fess point. This charge is known as " Foi." Faith, or brotherly love, may be displayed in the form of a fess, right across the field ; in bend, the arms coming from dexter chief and sinister base ; or in chevron, the arms bent and the hand clasped in the honour point. Crespin bore : sable, two arms issuing from the flanks and embowed in fess (to form a chevron), argent, hands conjoined in honour point, between three crescents of the second. De la Foy had two arms, en chevron, the hands grasping a heart ; while Purefoy, Bishop of Hereford, 1554–7, bore : gules, two arms issuing from flanks, hands conjoined in fess, argent, between three hearts, or. Later Purefoys and Purfeys varied this by bearing respectively : gules, three pairs of hands back to back, argent ; gules, three pairs of hands couped and clasped, argent ; sable, six armed hands clasped argent ; and sable, three pairs of dexter hands couped or, suffled argent.

Legs are treated much in the same way as arms. They may be naked, habited, or covered in chain mail or plate armour. They are seen as charges and as crests, and appear on the coats of Legges. Tramail, of Devon, bears : argent, a fess between three feet gules. A curious coat is that of the Italian Bones-Combas, wherein we see two legs issuing from the flanks, the feet bathing in the sea in base. Then we have the three naked bent legs, joined at the hips, and arranged in a triangle, on the arms of Sicily, the three-cornered Trinacria. This is an extremely ancient symbol of the swift-travelling sun of old-world meteorology. In some of the earliest examples we see a figure of the sun placed at the conjuncture of the three legs. This same symbol is found on the shield of the Isle of Man, only here the legs are in armour, and armed with spurs. At first the armour was of the chain-mail order, then of plates. No doubt this modification of the Mediterranean symbol was introduced into Man by descendants of the Norman Kings of Sicily. The Courtins of France bore : three naked legs in triangle, conjoined at the thighs, together with a doe tripping, which appears something like tautology, unless it meant that the bearer was swift of foot in hunting.

This idea of swiftness is associated with the foot, which is sometimes borne with two wings issuing from the shinbone, or from the sandal of Mercury strapped thereon.

ARMS OF READING.

CHAPTER IX

CELESTIAL CHARGES

R EPRESENTATIONS of heavenly bodies and phenomena
were early used alike in universal symbolism and in
heraldic art.

Heralds depict the sun as " rayonnant," " in splendour,"
and in this they followed very ancient precedents, for in
most corners of the world we find the solar disc surrounded
by lambent or darting rays. For the most part, these are
so arranged as to convey a notion of forward or rotary
motion. On the platter found by Edward Muller in the
undated ruins of Rhodesia among the astronomical signs is a
sun image, consisting of a circle surrounded by wedge-shaped
rays, curving from right to left, thus giving it the appearance
of a wheel or flower. In the ancient badge of Sicily we see
a human-faced disc placed at the conjunction of three bent
naked legs. This latter is a form of the cramponed cross, or
fylfot, of which more has been noted in another chapter ; but
it is to be said that both the cramponed cross and the three
conjoined bent legs (sun symbols) are recognised charges in
heraldry. Marduk, the Chaldean and Babylonian solar god,
was represented by a winged disc. So was his Persian descendant, Mithra, *Soli invicto Mithræ*, worshipped practically
throughout the Roman Empire. But long before that Ra
and Amen Ra in Egypt were also solar gods, and were worshipped in their material phase represented by Aten, the
solar disc. This, too, was often winged, or twined about by
winged snakes. Aten is also represented as emitting beneficent rays, sometimes shown in the form of small triangular
wedges strung together like the tail of a kite, but often even

more significantly represented as long beams terminating in human hands, spread out in the act of blessing. This idea of the arm and hand issuing forth from the heavens is also the common property of heralds. The University of Paris bears : azure, three fleurs-de-lis or, a hand and arm issuing from clouds in chief holding a book. Much the same symbolism is adopted by our College of Physicians. But these heavenly gifts may be crowns, swords or battle-axes as well as books.

A sun in splendour in later heraldry often has a human face, and the rays may be straight or wavy, of equal length all round, forming a fringe to the circle, or of varying length, so as to produce a fringe having the form of a diamond. The sun in splendour, as we shall see, was a badge of the House of Tudor, and was subsequently charged with a Tudor rose. It is also connected with another flower, the sun-flower, heliotrope or girasole, which always turns its full blossom towards the luminary, generally placed in dexter chief. Suns are occasionally charged, as with the rose ; they are also shown as sable discs, and are then said to be " in eclipse." The Oriental method of representing an eclipse is to show a dragon endeavouring to swallow the disc, as in the Chinese Imperial dragon, which has its two jaw feelers curved round the golden or red sun. Delahay bore : argent, the sun in splendour or ; and John de Fontibus, Bishop of Ely, 1280–5 : azure, the sun and moon in chief and seven stars in base all or. The town of Banbury : azure, a sun in splendour, or. The feudal coat of the lordship of Cardross was : gules, an eagle displayed or, looking towards the sun in its splendour in dexter chief. A sky with a radiant golden sun was borne by the French Solanges, and the Dutch Zon as armes parlantes. The German Counts Sonnenberg for the same reason bear : azure, the sun or, in base a mountain gold ; and the Scottish Hills have : azure, a sun rising from behind a hill or.

Sunrays themselves are borne, either as single charges or in connection with clouds. One of Richard II's favourite badges was a " cloudburst " (a sun behind clouds, sending forth rays). Rauf de la Hay (*temp*. Henry III) bore : argent, a sunray gules ; but as we have seen above this ultimately developed into a sun in splendour. Sir Francis de Aldom (*temp*. Edward II) : azure, a sunray or. Another interesting coat is described as : gules, a chief argent, on lower part a cloud with golden rays proceeding therefrom. The clouds are sometimes replaced by a chief nebulé.

A full moon is said to be " in her complement," and is generally represented as silver, with a human face, and surrounded by short rays. Day picturesquely bore : gules, two flanches ermine, on a chief azure, a sun between two moons or.

Both in symbolism and in heraldry the crescent is more commonly met with than the full moon. This is due, in the first instance, to the striking phenomena of the waning and waxing of that celestial body. All over the world the waxing moon was associated with fertility and prosperity. According to the ancient Indian legend, the moon was a receptacle of nectar, which the gods drained, when she dwindled and lost her beneficial influence. But the sun replenished her, and then in her march to fulness she brought plenty to all her followers. It was, therefore, the symbol of acceptable and efficacious sacrifice, and as such was the badge of Siva, " Lord of the Mountains." It was the symbol of certain elemental gods of the Egyptians and was also the attribute of Diana, as well as several deities of the Mediterranean basin. In Egyptian symbology the crescent moon is often shown as containing the disc within its horns—the present containing the promise of the future. In heraldry it is said to be a " crescent " when on its back, " increscent " when the horns are towards the dexter ; and " decrescent " when turned to the sinister. We find the increscent and decrescent endorsed ; the three endorsed ; or the three interlaced. Gimball, France, bears : azure, three crescents interlaced in triangle or ; which was the device of Henry II of France, in fond allusion to Diane de Poitiers. Lunel, also from across the Channel, has four crescents in cross. It was by accident that the crescent became the Mahomedan cognisance, for it was adopted only after the capture of Constantinople, where they found the Byzantine crescent so largely used. It had been adopted by the Byzantine Emperors because it was the long recognised symbol of Keröessa, "the horned"

HAWK GOD WITH THE SOLAR DISC WITHIN THE CRESCENT MOON.

daughter of the moon goodess Jö or Hera. It is possible that many of the crescents in our early heraldry may have been brought back by the Crusaders. The idea of the cross surmounting the crescent was neatly pictured by Cathcart, who bears : azure, three cross-crosslets fitchy rising from as many crescents argent. On the other hand it is very certain that it was used here symbolically quite early, either through Roman influence in Britain, or indirectly through the Germanic tribes. We find the crescent on the coins of our early Saxon kings, generally placed on the king's forehead, a circular disc being shown between the horns, as in the Egyptian examples. This appears to represent the Alpha and Omega, Day and Night, Eternity.

Stars, however, are more frequently seen associated with the crescent. Here, again, the Turkish analogy is a late accident, for they adopted their symbolism from other and older civilisations. On the Kokip Sesvators, or sacrificial stone of the North West Indian tribes of Canada (found near the Deer River), and supposed to have been used by the ancestors of the Toltecs, there is sculptured on the surface " half an inch deep, the crescent figure of the moon with a shining star over it." This same combination is seen on a Roman medal (figured by Vulson de Colombière) showing the deathly tribute of the Sabines to the betrayer of Rome. We find it used by our Plantagenet line of kings on their Great Seals, evidently as religious emblems, and by Richard I as a badge. On the quaint old seal of the town of Wareham we find a crescent with a star within its horns, between three fleurs-de-lis reversed. The town of Portsmouth bears : azure, an estoile issuing from a crescent argent. Stars, or " estoiles," are borne apart from the crescent. Stars appear on coins of Cunobeline, king of the Trinobantes, and we find them on the coins of our first Norman kings, either William I or William II. They are there placed within a circle or on a disc. In heraldry there is some confusion between the mullet and the estoile, but it may be assumed that the pierced charge is really a spur-rowel, while the same figure, with five, six, eight or more points, when borne wavy, or the points alternating wavy and straight, are stars. This waviness was adopted to represent the lambent aspect, or "twinkling" of the stars, an effect resulting from the refractive power of our atmosphere. It is a device which has given rise to some confusion, for

often there is a great resemblance between the daisy-like
flower (probably the rose) of our early seals and the equally
ancient star. This mingling of characteristics, however, is
not unusual in symbolism. Gale Pedrick in his " Monastic
Seals of the Thirteenth Century " says : " Ethiluwald,
Bishop of Dunwich (an extinct episcopate), who swayed the
crozier A.D. 845–70, used a bronze matrix dstinguished by
an ornamental star of eight points, alternately leaf-shaped
and fleury, with his name and description." This seems akin
to the Egyptians, who identified Isis (Sirius) the morning
star, with the rising of the fertilising waters of the Nile.
Their star of five points, however, seems to have represented
the united powers of the planets Mars, Mercury, Jupiter,
Saturn and Venus. Probably the pentacle had the same
planetary significance. De Burbentane-Puget (Provence)
bore : argent, a cow passant guardant gules, and between
the horns a star or ; which seems quite suggestive of the
horn-crowned Egyptian cow goddess Hathor. Gilbert Han-
sarde (temp. Henry III), bore : gules, three estoiles argent.
An " illegitimate " but very beautiful coat is that of Conti,
Florence : per pale azure and bleue celeste, an estoile counterchanged. Pale sky blue is very rare in heraldry, except
when used for flags, but it is found in the arms of the Kingdom
of Greece. Sir Francis Drake bore : sable, a fess wavy between
two polar stars argent.

The star of Bethlehem is usually an estoile of many points
with rays projecting from the lower part. The Beaux of
Luxembourg bore : gules, a comet star of sixteen rays,
argent. They claimed to be descendants of Balthasar, one
of the three kings, or Magi, who saw the star over Bethlehem
from the mountain of Beaulx in India ; whence they journeyed
to the Holy City, and thence to Cologne.

Both Australia and New Zealand have adopted the constellation of the Southern Cross. In the fly of the Commonwealth flag the constellation is represented by four large
stars of seven rays, and a smaller one of five rays, while
there is a large seven-pointed star beneath the Jack. In
the Commonwealth arms the cross is charged with four stars

with eight points, while over the blue field of the second quarter of the quartered shield the constellation is represented by one silver star of eight points, two of seven, one of six and one of five points. Victoria bears : azure the Southern Cross, represented by three large and one small silver stars. On the New Zealand blazonry the constellation is represented by four silver stars surmounted by as many red stars, on a blue field. The United States of America bear : paly of thirteen gules and argent, on a chief azure forty-eight stars of five points argent. A " comet " or " blazing star " is usually " bearded " or " coudé," that is to say, represented with a trail of rays forming a slanting tail. De Blacas, of Provence, bears : argent a comet bearded of sixteen rays gules. But Vulson gives the following strange blazon for Rabot of the Dauphiné : argent, three piles flamboyant and two comets gules. These figures are diminutives of the pile, three of them being reversed.

Rainbows are represented by a bend bowed of azure, gules, gold and sometimes argent, the colours subdued and blending one with another. Pont, of Scotland, bears : argent, a rainbow in fess proper. Claret : azure, a rainbow in fess proper, between two estoiles in chief and the sun in base, or. Barons Pfuhl, however, have three rainbows in pale on a blue field.

Clouds have already been mentioned in connection with the sun and sunrays. They are, however, also borne as an orle or bordure, for instance in the arms of the Mercers' Company. Frequently they are shown as a bank out of which an arm or other charge may issue. The tinctures are argent and azure. Azure, three clouds radiated in base or, each surmounted by a triple crown gold, lined gules, are the arms of the Drapers' Guild, London. Leeson, Earls of Milltown, Ireland, bear: gules, a chief argent, in base thereof a cloud proper, issuant therefrom rays of light paleways or. Tempesta, of Italy : gules, eleven hailstones argent.

In ancient Egyptian carvings the welcome rain is represented by a figure much like our label with two points, one

7

at each end, and streaming from the lower side a series of chevroné or, less frequently, wavy lines.

Thunderbolts are borne as ordinary charges and also held in the talons of birds or paws of beasts. They are in the form of short double-headed voluted staves, with forked and barbed lines issuing from them, often flaming at each end, and winged. They represent meteorites, conventionalised into double sceptres. These are the " bolts from the blue," the darts of outraged divinities which punished, yet brought blessings in their train. For while observation showed that both lightning and meteorites could kill, yet, being associated with vernal thunderstorms, brought revivifying rains. Meteorites have ever been considered sacred and lucky in all countries. There is the black Kaaba at Mecca ; the thunderbolt of Indra at Sambundth. In Mexico the Aztecs had a god Tecpatl (Flint-stone) who fell from the sky and broke into 1,600 gods. The Greeks and Romans showed Jove and Jupiter hurling thunderbolts, and their eagles carried the dread sceptres in their claws, hence their appearance in the talons of the Imperial eagles of Rome and France, and of the American bird of prey. Tomyris bears : azure, a thunderbolt or, shafted, and winged argent. A similar charge is the crest of the Carnegies, Earls of Southesk.

CHAPTER X

COMMON CHARGES

APART from the two classes of ordinaries discussed in the preceding chapters almost every conceivable object in the sky, on the earth and beneath the sea has been utilised at one time or another as a charge for an armorial shield.

Naturally, the earliest employed were either of a conventional order, developments of structural members of shields, ancient symbols, or those things particularly associated with warfare, or the possession of land and all that it entailed. Then,

MERCHANT'S MARK,
JOHN CARLTON,
NORWICH,
15TH CENTURY.

MERCHANT'S MARK,
ADAM DE MUNDHAM,
NORWICH,
16TH CENTURY.

MERCHANT'S MARK,
JOHN DE AUBRY,
NORWICH,
14TH CENTURY.

with the expansion of our own social system, came many new interests ; this is reflected in armoury by the introduction of objects connected with travel, with professions and trades, for merchants' marks early assumed heraldic form. While it would serve no useful purpose to give a list of every single charge ever emblazoned on a shield, the principal classes employed will be considered here, as far as possible in the order just given.

Of the developed structural part of the shield, escarbuncles, fers-de-moline and staples are of chief importance. The escar-

99

buncle may be described as a central boss with eight radiating limbs, treated, as in the beautiful example in the Temple Church, as foliated branches, or as a series of decorated sceptres. Sometimes these members are united by one or more series of decorated transverse bars. This was obviously the appropriate kind of decorative ironwork for lending

FONTENAY-SOUS-BOIS, PARIS.
AN ESCARBUNCLE IN CHIEF.

strength to a shield, and something similar may often be seen on old wooden church doors. At first it was a mere ornament and had no armorial significance, for we see it, as in the Temple Church example, sprawling over the three dancetté bars of the coat. Later, however, it was treated as a charge, and called a carbuncle, or rich ruby, sending forth blinding rays. The most famous examples of this bearing are the following :
Counts of Cleve : gules, on an inescutcheon argent, an escarbuncle flory or ; which was changed later to : argent, an escarbuncle or, over all an inescutcheon sable. Counts of Anjou : gules, a chief argent, over all an escarbuncle or. Abbey of St. John, Colchester : gules, a cross within a border or, over all an escarbuncle of eight points sable.

Fers-de-moline, or millrines, are variously drawn, but consist essentially of two outwardly curving members, conjoined at the back. They are like the clamps sometimes used to anchor a beam in a wall. In the fanciful minds of the fifteenth-century heralds they are supposed to denote certain seigneural rights, the privilege of owning mills. Fers-de-molines are extensively used. Sir William Saunsum (*temp*. Edward II) bore : or, a fer-de-moline, sable ; and Sir Robert de Willoughby is described in the Roll of Arms of the same period as bearing ; gules, a fer-de-moline argent. Molyner, with allusive intent, bore : or, a fer-de-moline azure.

Staples of the ordinary form are borne. Stapleton has : argent, three staples sable. The arms of the Priory of

Dunstable, Bedfordshire, were : argent, on a pile sable a staple affixed to the centre, interlaced with a horse-shoe or. In other words, a horseshoe is fastened by a double nail to the pile.

Warfare supplies us with a multitude of charges.

Spears and lances appear at quite an early date. They are usually of the heavy type, with large head and sunk hand grip. Six of these appear to form a fretty field on the coat of de Villeneuve, as already mentioned. Saint Vincent, also of Provence, had two gold lances on a field of gules. But the most interesting specimen is that on the arms granted in 1546 to the father of William Shakespeare, of Stratford-on-Avon : or, on a bend sable a spear of the field, headed argent. Spear-heads also are borne. Pryce, of Wales, has : sable, three spear-heads argent. Lance-heads of the jousting weapon, with its four blunt points, are called coronels. In later time spears of another kind, such as those of the American Indian, the African warrior, the Zulu assagai, have appeared to record war services or administration in our colonies.

Swords are also of various types. The falchion was a blade shaped like an elongated triangle. Knightly swords are long, straight, with prominent cross-guard handles. Scimitars have broad curved blades, serrated at the back towards the top. Seaxes, the ancient Scandinavian sword, is also curved, and has a notch in the back of the blade. It may be seen in the arms used by the county authorities of Middlesex and Essex. Naval cutlasses, Scottish basket-handled claymores, modern cavalry sabres, skenes or daggers are also seen. They may be " hilted " of any tincture. Swords may be borne in their scabbards, when they are said to be " sheathed "; the metal end-piece of the scabbard is a " chape," " crampet " or " boterole," which may be differently tinctured and is sometimes borne as a separate charge. Dymock bears : sable, a sword erect in pale, hilt and pomel or (a badge of office as King's Champion). Gelli-brand (*temp.* Henry VIII) : argent, two swords sheathed in saltire, hilts and chapes or. Becheton : azure, three chapes or. In ecclesiastical heraldry it is the symbol of spiritual and temporal authority, but more generally an emblem of martyrdom, as borne by the see of London : gules, two swords in saltire, argent, hilted or, the points in chief, in allusion to St. Paul who suffered by decapitation.   Battle-axes are among the weapons.

Bows are borne bent (" stringed ") and unbent.   They led up to the cross-bow, the musket and the rifle.   Gun bears allusively, but perhaps also emblematically, having regard to the chief : gules, two muskets in saltire sable, within a border argent ; on a chief or, a lion passant guardant of the field.

Arrows appear singly, in " sheaf " (or bundles), and sometimes, though rarely, in quivers or cases.   When the head or feathering is of a different tincture to the shaft, it is said to be " barbed " or " flighted " of the special colour or metal.   The city of Sheffield bears : vert, three wheatsheaves or, on a chief azure eight golden arrows in saltire, banded silver ; and for crest, a lion rampant gorged with a collar azure, holding in its paws an escutcheon azure, charged with eight arrows as in the chief.   These arrows, of course, recall the iron and steel industry and the former important local production of arrow-heads.   Sometimes they are shown with blunted or cross-headed points, and are then known as " bird bolts."   A peculiar form of the arrow-head is the " pheon."   It is like a broad arrow, but with the inner sides of the barbs serrated.   Gules, three arrows double pointed or, is borne by Hales.   Or, a pheon azure, were the arms of Sydney, Earls of Leicester.

We have also slings and catapults, battering-rams, cannon, hand grenades, chain and bar shot as well as cannon-balls. The calthrop is a ball with four spikes, so that, however thrown, one would remain uppermost ; they were used to disorganise cavalry.

Warfare also provides us with helmets, shields, gauntlets (azure, three gauntlets or, as borne by Vane), men in armour, spurs, stirrups, bridles, horses in armour, and much besides.   The Wardens of the Marshes bore crests or badges of winged spurs to show their readiness for action.

Annulets, or thick rings, seem to be borne both as pieces

of chain armour and also as the tilting-rings. In the former aspect they are sometimes borne " conjunct " or " conjoined," when two are united at their edges, and " embraced," or " interlaced," one link fitting into another.   Gules, four annulets or, was borne by Sir Nicholas de Cromwell in the days of Edward II.

WINGED SPUR CREST.

Buckles should also be mentioned in this connection.   They were borne both alone and attached to belts.   Doubtless sometimes they were merely emblematic, but occasionally they were assumed to commemorate prowess in the field. This was the case in the well-known Pelham buckle borne as a badge and on the shield : gules, two half belts palewise in fess, the buckles in chief argent.   These were assumed by Sir John de Pelham to commemorate the part he took in the capture of King John of France at Poitiers.

Horse trappings include the barnacle, bray or twitchers, used for training (azure, three pairs of barnacles expanded in pale, sable, is borne by Bray of Cornwall), hames (or collars), and, of course, horseshoes.   Another of these equine charges is the celebrated fetterlock, not unlike a single manacle or handcuff, a semi-circle closed by a chain and padlock.   This is constantly used as a charge, a crest and a badge alone and in conjunction with some other object.   It is one of the Yorkist badges used by Henry VII, with whom it was made to enclose a white falcon, though his successor opened the lock.   It occurs in a curious combination in the arms of the town of Bewdley : argent, an anchor azure, ringed argent, interlaced with a closed fetterlock of the second ; within the fetterlock on the dexter side of the anchor shaft a blue sword erect, on the sinister side a rose gules. Scaling-ladders are also used.

Directly connected with the gentle art of killing fellow creatures are two interesting pieces indispensable in victualling armies. The first of these is the water-bowget reminiscent of the Crusading days, and representing in a

BOROUGH OF CLERKENWELL.
CREST: WATER-BOWGET SUR-
MOUNTED BY BOW AND ARROW.
WATER BOWGET IN FOURTH
QUARTER.

highly conventionalised form the animal skins used in place of barrels to convey water and other liquids. These appear quite early on mediæval shields. A notable instance is that of William de Ross (*temp.* Henry III), who bore: gules, three water bowgets argent. Trusbutt, in the reign of Edward III, also had three of these charges. Curiously enough the other commissariat charge, a great cauldron, appears on the shield of Mount-bourchier, as shown on the cloister ceiling of Canterbury Cathedral. Possibly there, as in the case of the Italian Pignatello, the cooking-pot may be allusive, in the sense of a pun on the names. But with the De Laras and other grandees of Spain it was allusive to feudal position as great princes and leaders of men. It was borne by them as a symbol of their right to levy armies, and some of them placed eels in their pots. In

ARMS OF THE DE CONCHA-CHAVES OF SPAIN.

HERALDIC PENDANT

the same way both on the Continent and in England, nobles who raised troops often bore banners as charges or as crests. Sometimes these were badges of office, as with the Bannermans of Scotland. Banners are, of course, mainly allusive to war. But the gonfanon type, that is, a banner attached to a crossbar, which is slung horizontally across the staff, is ecclesiastical. Of old every ecclesiastical establishment and every parish had its banner, and on the Continent at least these were borne by the lay protectors, the avoués, or advocates of the foundations, who not infrequently added representations of these banners to their arms, either on the shield or attached to the helm or in the hands of the supporters.

An important group relates to buildings, the most prominent sub-sections consisting of towers and castles. A tower generally has one doorway, called a " port," which may be closed by a door or a gate, " portcullis." The top is always " crenelated," otherwise " embattled," but occasionally one, two or three small towers may spring from the top. The town of Newcastle bears : gules, three towers argent. The town of Morpeth bears : argent, three bars gules, within a border azure, charged with eight martlets or ; over all a tower triple-towered, of the field. Castles usually consist of a strip of crenelated wall between two towers ; an arched " port " in the centre, and one in each tower, and four oval windows. If there are three towers, the centre is the tallest. This is the type seen on the ancient seal of the town of Winchester : gules, five triple-towered castles in saltire argent, the middle castle between two lions of England confronté. That is to say, the dexter golden lion passant guardant is turned to the sinister. Edinburgh City bears : argent a triple tower sable, masoned silver, port, windows and flags gules. Dublin bears : azure, three castles argent, with signal flames issuing from the towers. Exeter has a curious castle : per pale gules and sable, a triangular triple-towered castle or. For crest the city of Cambridge has on a green mount a quadrangular castle, with four domed towers and two ports or, masoned sable. The

arms of the ancient castle town of Guildford deserve record.
On a black shield is a green mount supporting a silver castle
of two embattled towers, each having a spire surmounted
by a ball. From the battlement between the end towers
springs a triple-towered tower, charged with a small shield
bearing quarterly the arms of France modern (*i.e.*, blue with
three fleurs-de-lis, two above and one below) and England
(*i.e.*, red with three gold lions passant guardant, one above
the other). Under the battlements of the castle are two golden
roses ; in the centre of the black doorway are a key and portcullis in gold. On the mount before the doorway is a golden
lion couchant affronté. On each side of the castle is a silver
woolpack. Blue water occupies the lower part of the shield.
This appears to be an adoption of the ancient corporation
seal, and is fully descriptive of the physical and political
position of the town and of its commercial activity as an
olden wool centre. Towers and castles appear frequently on
personal arms. De la Tour d'Auvergne (whence sprang the
celebrated mid-seventeenth century Marshal de Turenne)
quite early bore : gules, a tower with portcullis close, argent.
In 1191, however, they bore : azure, a tower argent. In
1222 they powdered the field with fleurs-de-lis. De Castel-
lane, of Provence, bore : gules, a castle of three towers or ;
which was allusive to his name and the office which gave
him his name. Another allusive use of this charge is in the
celebrated castles of the Kingdom of Castile, still to be seen
quartered with lions of Leon and the pomegranate of Granada
in the arms of Spain.

The term " masoned " is applied to the picking out of
the masonry courses in a tincture distinct from that of the
building. The city of Bath bears : per fess embattled azure
and gules, the base masoned sable, with crosses bottoné of
the last (really loopholes), in chief two bars wavy argent,
over all in pale a sword silver, pommelled gold. In the
arms of the city of Cambridge the embowed gold fess is
masoned sable and triple towered, and as it spans water with
three barges thereon, no doubt represents a bridge. Bridges
of two or more arches are occasionally found. Pount bore

(allusively) : azure, a bridge of two arches argent. For the same reason Arches bore : gules, three arches, two single in chief, one double in base, argent, imposts or. Ruins appear on the shield of Bertie, quartered with battering-rams, which looks very warlike, but, as a matter of fact, the founder of the family was not only Captain of Castles in Sussex, but a contractor for their construction and repair. In the same spirit George Cubitt, Lord Ashcombe, the famous builder-contractor, emblazoned his shield, chequy or and gules, to represent brickwork, and had for supporters a mason and a carpenter. Mansard, Louis XIV's celebrated architect, had a silver pillar resting on a gold pedestal. Some charges, and many ordinaries, as well as partitions of the field, may be borne " crenellé," " embattled," or " crenelated."

Churches are emblazoned, but mostly in connection with ecclesiastical armoury. Of recent years lighthouses have been introduced into heraldry, chiefly as crests in connection with seaports, as at Broadstairs.

Castle gates, known as portcullis (from *porte coulis*, sliding door), or *herse*, is a frequent charge. It was one of the cherished badges of the House of Tudor, who derived it from their ancestors, the Beauforts. It is in the form of a grid, the cross bars being nailed at the junctions. Frequently chains are borne pendent on each side. The port of Harwich bore : gules, a portcullis or (now argent), cloué azure.

Keys may, not inappropriately, be mentioned here, for, though sometimes having a religious significance, they are for the most part connected with problems of defence. In the latter sense we find them significantly associated with castles on the armorial shields of Gibraltar and the town of Totnes. Gibraltar bears : gules, a triple-towered castle on a rock argent, the port opened, and pendent therefrom by a chain, a key with ward downwards or. Totnes bears : sable, a castle with central crenelated tower and two flanking domed turrets argent, masoned sable, the port open, between two silver keys, wards in chief and pointing outwards. The island of Mauritius, another strategical key, has for its fourth quarter azure, a key or. De Clermont-Tonnerre, France, Dukes and Counts of Clermont, Grand Masters and Constables of the Dauphiné, bore : gules, two keys argent in saltire. In Spain we find the Counts of Herrera de la Concha-Chaves, hereditary supervisors of Government buildings, having in base : or, five keys azure. Wood of Balbigno, Scotland, bears : azure, an oaktree growing out of mount in base or, pendent from a branch two keys gold, fastened by a strap gules. These keys are the badge of office as Thane of Fetter-cairn. Keys were used as badges of office, usually placed outside the shield, by Chamberlains at the French Court. From German sources we find quaint key combinations. Beheim bears : gules, a triangle or, thereon are threaded the rings of three golden keys, the barrels and wards pointed to dexter and sinister chief and the third borne in pale. Liedlow bears : azure, three keys argent, rings interlaced in chief point, the barrels and wards pointing to dexter and sinister chief and in base. In the religious sense keys were valued badges of the Moslems, for they bore allusion to the Kaaba and the Koran. They were largely used for decorative-symbolical purposes by the Moors in Spain. In Christian iconography a key is the emblem of St. Peter, and the Popes of Rome as successors of the Apostle assumed keys as their badge, using two crossed in saltire to represent their spiritual and temporal powers. Through Rome, singly and crossed in saltire, they are constantly seen in our own ecclesiastical heraldry.

Seafaring has enriched our armoury to a large extent, apart from the interesting family of fish, beasts and curious fowl already described. First of all we have the sea itself, which may be painted *au naturelle*, or " proper " as the heralds have it, or symbolically represented by blue and silver wavy bars. Then we have a ghostly fleet of strange craft. Foremost among these is the lymphad, or ancient galley. It is usually depicted as a half-moon, with castellated poop and stern, with or without mast, and with one or more banks of sweeps, or oars. This form is seen on some of the early shields. It is frequently met with in Scottish heraldry, especially in connection with the coastal and island clans. It was the feudal ensign of the lordship of Lorne.

In heraldry ships almost invariably refer to sea dominion, warfare, exploring and commerce, but occasionally they have a religious reference, for in Christian iconography a ship represents the sheltering Church, which was derived from Noah's Ark, essentially the symbol of refuge. The Ark is seen as the crest of the London Shipwrights' Guild, with the dove alighting with its olive-branch. This ship of refuge, however, is a very old notion, found in many countries. In Egypt raft boats were sacred to Ra, who made his diurnal journey round the world in three boats. One was the " Boat of a Million Years," and as it passed through Tuat, or the Underworld, the souls of those who had passed the moat-test, were taken on board, and with Ra journeyed to the Elysian Fields. When Isis was seeking

SCHWANN, BARONETS. AZURE, A SWAN ROUSANT PROPER WITHIN AN ORLE OF LYMPHADS OR.

for the scattered members of slaughtered Osiris, she made a boat of papyrus, which was permitted to go unmolested by all the beasts and fishes. To commemorate this there was a feast of boats at Denderah, when thirty-four boats, lit by

365 lamps, were launched. In Japan there is a feast of
boats, when small boys launch paper and straw boats with
tapers alight. In New Granada the Spaniards found that
the Casique El Dorado, glittering with precious metal, went
on a raft on the boisterous water of a big lake to cast
offerings therein. So the Doge of Venice sailed on his
golden galley, throwing a golden ring into the waves in
token of the marriage of the city to the sea.

A great number of our seaport towns have ancient ships
on their shields, many of them having been transferred from
symbolic but non-armorial seals, as in the case of Scarborough and Hythe, the latter having one man blowing on
a horn, while two naked sailors are lying on the yard-
arms, apparently furling sails, while fish swim in the sea.
This crowded ship of Hythe is very close to the community
emblem, which we find again in the city of Paris arms, which
an old poem describes as manned by representative citizens.
We find ancient ships on the seals and arms of the corporations
of Winchelsea, Dunwich, Lymington, Aldborough, Ipswich,
Yarmouth, Oxford, Newport, Truro, Bristol, and others.
The curious lion-ships created by the dimidiation of the royal
arms with those of the Cinque Ports and other seaside towns
have already been mentioned. At Weymouth we have a
Tudor man-of-war, a Great Harry. Since Manchester became
a port, a three-masted trading vessel under full sail has been
added on a chief ; while at Govan we have a ship's hull on
the building-stocks. Other types include men-of-war of
different periods, rowing-boats and even coracles.

But sea power is represented variously. We have the
anchor (which, however, is also frequently the symbol of
Hope of Christian iconography). Anchors may have the
flukes, the cross bar (" stock " or " timber ") and the ring
of tinctures varying from that of the shaft (" shank " or
" beam "), and may be borne " cabled." When the cable
is wound round the anchor it is said to be " foul," and this
is the form in which it is used as a badge of the Admiralty.
A curious use of the anchor has already been cited in the
case of Bewdley. The anchor entwined by a dolphin is one

of the sea-power and religious symbols of the classic ages, and was adopted by the early Christians as an emblem of Hope and Resurrection.

Oars are borne singly and crossed in saltire. Silver oars are badges used by the English Admiralty Courts, and many ancient sea-ports have silver oars borne before their mayors in addition to the civic mace, in token of their naval jurisdiction. Rudders are also used in a somewhat similar sense, again a symbolism which has come down to us from classic times, as may be seen on referring to old monuments and coins. The trident of Neptune is also a symbol of naval power, and is sometimes seen wreathed with a dolphin. On the exergus of the counter-seal of George IV, we see a rudder of the Roman type. On the Great Seal of William IV, the background represents the sea, with two lines of battleships, while on the exergus is a trident ensigned with a wreath of laurel, and on the counter-seal Neptune, bearing his trident, appears amid an allegorical group. The top part of a trident surrounded by laurel-branches appears on the exergus of Queen's Victoria's Great Seal.

Landscape shields, which are pictorial rather than heraldic, belong to the bad period, from the seventeenth century to the middle of the nineteenth. But conventionalised features of landscapes, to represent territorial dominion or origin, were introduced quite early. Mention has already been made of castles and beasts standing on mounts, even of a representation of Mount Parnassus. However, mountains alone are frequent charges. They form quite a feature of Scottish heraldry, representing the lordships of clan chieftains. In some cases the mountains are represented as crested with lurid flames, these being intended as war fire signals. But the flaming mountains are singularly like the conventionalised Japanese figures of smoking Mount Fujiyama, and many antiquaries have seen in the Scottish fire mountains survivals of clan badges telling of former vicinity to volcanoes, either local or Scandinavian. Mountains are also favourite charges on the Continent, both on municipal and knightly shields. In Italian and Provençal heraldry the mountains are usually drawn as high and steep. This is the characteristic of the sea-washed triple hill of Nice, straddled by the Lascaris eagle. De Meyronnet, of Provence, bears : azure, a mount issuing from the sea, and two crescents in chief argent. In English heraldry small hills, generally crowned by a group of trees, and known as " hursts," are more commonly met with. Our " parks " are really circular palings on a green terrace, and may enclose trees, harts or other animals. " Islands " are patches of green, circular in form, floating on the sea or on the field, and may grow trees. This type of island, crowned by palms, is seen on the shield granted to Christopher Columbus, but as a rule in Spanish, as in most other Continental countries, islands are represented by high, rocky hills, surrounded by the sea, as on the shields of the Pinzons, Columbus's one-time lieutenants. In modern practice more elaborate landscapes were admitted, as in the flower-bed mount of the Montefiores ; the ranges of small mountains, green hills of wheatfield of Alberta ; and the mountains and plain of Natal.

Of the component parts of landscapes, such as trees and wheatsheaves, much has to be said, and will be reserved for a separate chapter. Other charges connected with the countryside may be briefly reviewed. Sickles or reaping-hooks appear in British heraldry. A sickle was the famous badge of the Hungerfords, and was also the crest of the Dukes of Brunswick, who usually adorned the outer edge with a row of eyes from peacock feathers. Sicklemore bears : sable, three sickles interwoven, argent. Mayere, of Flanders, bore : gules, three sickles argent, handles gold, the points meeting in fess. Scythes also appear. Argent, a scythe sable, is borne by Snelson. They are also shown in the hands of men forming part of crests, or standing as supporters. Flails when borne are also usually held in men's hands. Land suggests sport, which has endowed heraldry with many birds, beasts and fishes. Hawks' lures and bells, and bird bolts have already been mentioned. Hunting-horns are favourite charges. They are of the bullock-horn type, with mouth-piece, which may be of a special tincture, and is then said

EXAMPLES OF COMMON CHARGES.

I. BARBER-SURGEONS' GUILD, ROPERS' GUILD   II. CARPENTERS', JOINERS', COOPERS', WHEELWRIGHTS',
(DURHAM GUILDS).   SAWYERS' GUILDS.

to be "enguiché." We also have lobster-pots, nets, river weirs and fish-hooks. Of quiet forms of sport the quaintest are the chess-rooks, favourites in former days. Gules, three chess-rooks argent, was borne by Richard de Walsingham in the reign of Edward II. We also find dice and playing-cards.

From the wardrobe quite a long list of charges has been obtained. Perhaps the most striking and earliest of these is the maunch or manche, an old-fashioned sleeve, with long pendent cuff. Reinald de Mohun (*temp.* Henry III) bore : gules, a maunch argent. But his successor in the days of Edward III bore : gules, a maunch ermine ; and his descendant, the Earl of Somerset, bore : gules, a maunch ermine, a hand proper issuing therefrom holding a fleur-de-lis or. For very long, however, the maunch has been specially associated with Hastings, the head of whom in Edward III's time bore : or, a maunch gules. At a later period the Lincolnshire branch of the family bore : argent, a maunch sable. It has been conjectured that, at all events in the case of the Hastings family, the maunch was originally a badge of office, as we first hear of them as holding a post at Court corresponding to that of Master of the Household. Next we have the surcoat, which is borne particoloured and also heraldically emblazoned. We have already mentioned gauntlets and helmets, but we also find gloves, caps, hats and shoes. Some of these may have come in as badges. Most, however, owe their presence to the ambitions of traders or trading corporations. Dame Berners in her "Boke of Saint Albans" (1486) mentions a "cross-corded," which, she says, was first introduced, the baronial bearer thereof having formerly been a corder. However that may be, it is certain that the trading guilds early obtained armorial insignia ; even before that they

CROSS-CORDED.

adopted heraldically designed banners and common seals. Among the charges thereon were generally found some implement of trade. Thus our own trading guilds have introduced hats and hatbands, gloves, plumbers' rules, stair-

8

rails, or banisters, butchers' cleavers and poleaxes, shoes, shuttles, basket-makers' tools and so on. Similar guilds on the Continent were following the same practice. There is ample evidence that office-bearers in these guilds, when they rose to wealth and influence, introduced some part of the guild arms into their own personal bearings. And certainly from the sixteenth century onwards we find successful professional men and traders recalling the sources of their prosperity by more or less appropriate heraldic charges. John Pep, Master of the Barber-Surgeons' Company, who was Groom of the Privy Chamber and King's Barber to Henry VIII, placed two silver combs on his shield. Thus we have the scales and swords of justice introduced by lawyers, the pastoral staff of ecclesiastics, the Aesculapian sceptre entwined with one or two snakes of the physicians, the fleams, or curiously razor-like lances of the surgeons, woolpacks and fleeces of woolmongers and a great many other charges of a like character. We have also the goats of the Skinners' Guilds, and the ermine of the Edinburgh Guild of Furriers.

In English heraldry mirrors are rarely seen except in the hands of mermaids, but when borne have a mystic meaning, for the mirror was always an object of awe, a symbol of revelation of secret things. In Japan it is emblematic of creation, representing the rising sun over the sea. Combs, also closely associated with mermaids, curiously enough are fairly common as charges. They are of the double-toothed variety.

Woolpacks are seen on the shields of Guildford, Godalming (in past days great wool-growing districts) and Rochdale, a centre of the wool-manufacturing industry. A woolpack also appears on the arms of Staple Inn, London, formerly one of the free markets where merchant-adventurers traded. Woolpacks are seen on the shields of Lords Tweedmouth and Holden, both heads of Yorkshire woollen manufacturing families.

Bury bears a shield which happily represents local industry while remaining heraldic in character : quarterly, argent and azure, a cross parted and fretted counterchanged, between,

WEAVERS' GUILD, EDINBURGH.

FURRIERS' GUILD, EDINBURGH.

SKINNERS' GUILDS, LONDON AND
EDINBURGH.

BRIDPORT.

in first quarter, an anvil sable, in the second a fleece of or, in the third two shuttles in saltire with threads pendent silver, and in the fourth three culms of the papyrus-plant proper. For crest, a bee between two fructed slips of the cotton-plant. Thus the iron, the woollen, the cotton and paper industries, as well as commerce generally, are represented. In the modern arms of Bolton-le-Moors a shuttle represents the weaving industry introduced into that town by Philippa of Hainault, Consort of Edward III, and a mule spinning spindle recalls that its inventor, Samuel Crompton, was born there. Shuttles are found in the arms of the Ibbetsons and the Kay-Shuttleworths, both of which families have won fame and fortune in the weaving trades. The ancient borough of Bridport, bore : gules, a castle argent, the port close ; on each tower a fleur-de-lis or ; in chief a lion passant guardant and crowned of gold, in base barry wavy of eight argent and azure. Apparently, about the middle of the sixteenth century, the portcullis was drawn up, and in the open gateway three " coqs " or roper's hooks were introduced. They appeared there on the Visitation of William Henry, Clarencieux King

GOLDSMITHS' GUILD, EDINBURGH.
COVERED CUPS.

of Arms, in 1565, and were approved and allowed on a subsequent Survey in 1623. Now, for long ages Bridport was renowned for its manufacture of ropes, and Henry VIII granted a monopoly to the town for the supply of cordage to the King's Navy.

Bottles and cups may have been introduced from trade sources occasionally, but they are of ancient use as badges of office. Take, for instance, the cups in the arms of the Butlers, who held the post of Chief Butlers to the King in Ireland. Cupbearers have always been important personages, and Kings not only had their Court butlers, but similar officials in different parts of their domains, while princes and feudal chiefs also appointed such officers. These cups are usually of the long-stemmed goblet pattern. Bottles are of two varieties, flagons, and leather receptacles, flat bottomed and ended, with semi-circular upper part, not unlike foot-warmers. Brewers and vintners introduced barrels.

We also find a variety of baskets, open and closed. Pentney Priory, Norfolk, bore: gules, three covered wicker baskets or. Middle-

BREWERS' GUILD, LONDON. BARRELS AND SHEATHS OF BARLEY.

ton Abbey, Dorset: sable, three flat open baskets full of bread, argent. Winnowing-baskets, or vans, are seen as early as the reign of Edward II, when Sir Robert de Suens bore: " de azure a III vans de or " (Roll of Arms, *temp*. Edward II). Fish-baskets, not unlike lobster-pots, are another type, while the Basket Makers' Company, or Guild, place basket-maskers' tools on their shield and have an osier cradle for crest.

Books, open or closed, are often associated with seats of learning, as in the case of the Universities of Cambridge, Oxford, London, Paris and others, but also with trade, as in the case of the Stationers' Company and some personal arms.

Books and seats of learning naturally bring to mind scourges. They are not unknown to heraldry. Battuli of Bologna allusively (but let us hope not as a matter of official badge) bore: argent, a bend azure between two scourges, each of four cords ending in spiked balls, or. Croyland Abbey

bore : quarterly first and fourth, gules, three knives erect
in fess argent, handled or ; second and third, azure, three
scourges erect in fess or, with three lashes each. Swift, of
Scotland, bore : gules, three whips of three lashes each, argent.
For crest the Lords Stourton have a demi-monk, habited in
russet, wielding in his dexter hand a scourge of three knotted
lashes. Knotted cords here have an unpleasant meaning,
and so, to some extent, they have in that curious group of
charges, the family badge knots, of which something is said
in another chapter.

Music supplies us with many instruments, the harp, the
military trumpet and bugle, Apollo's lyre (as seen in the
crest of the Musicians' Company or Guild), the hunter's horn,
drums, cymbals, hautboys, flutes, fiddles and that strange
charge the clarion or rest. The upper part of this instrument
is somewhat like a set of Pan's pipes, but has a curved horn-
like handle. It has been described as a lance rest and
various other things, but is clearly a form of musical instrument.

A group of pear-shaped charges with wavy tails are named
" goutes." They are variously tinctured, and when of gold
are called goutes auré or d'or ; of silver, d'eau ; of gules, de
sang ; of azure, de larmes ; of black, de poix (or pitch) ;
of green, d'huile. They are sometimes borne singly or in
numbered groups, but usually powdered, or semée over the
field. When a goute is drawn reversed, tail uppermost, it
is termed an icicle.

A very doubtful group of charges are the mullets, which
often look like stars, for they are more frequently borne un-
pierced than not. Yet the word mullet is derived from the
French *molette,* and so they are usually taken to be spur-
rowels. In early heraldry they were described indiscrimin-
ately as " estoilles " and " molettes." De Vere, Earl of
Oxford (*temp.* Henry III), bore : quarterly or and gules,
a mullet silver in the first quarter ; but in the reign of Edward
III the contemporary de Vere was said to sport an " estoille."
Nicholas de Moeles (*temp.* Henry III) bore allusively :
" d'argent a deux barres de goules a trois molets en le chef

de goules " (Roll of Arms). Sir William de Harpendene (*temp.* Edward II) bore : argent, a mullet pierced, gules. In ordinary practice English mullets have five points and the French six points, but they may have many more.

CHAPTER XI

PLANTS AND FLOWERS

A WONDERFULLY lovely and varied garden has been planted by heralds of all nations during the long procession of years from the dawn of the twelfth century at least, for not only has the whole vegetable kingdom been put under contribution, but the nameless symbol makers of the remote past have also been drawn upon. Man became a worshipper of trees, seed plants, and flowers almost from the time he began to think, and remains so still. When we dip into art we find evidence of his linking the beautiful mystery of growing things bursting forth from the bosom of Mother Earth, with half-formed longings to peep into the unknown surrounding him, on all sides. This we shall see as we go along.

Trees are seen as single specimens or as groves, " hursts," which sometimes shelter men or hinds, but also from whence wild boar, lions and other destroying marauders emerge. Trees are borne " eradicated " (torn up by the roots), and " couped " (cut off smoothly), as stumps (generally with the reassuring presence of young sprouting twigs) and " fructed " (bearing fruit). Branches torn off are " snagged," and when roughly trimmed with projecting stumps along their whole length, they are " raguly " or " ragged." These " ragged " branches, or " staves," are often seen in cross, or saltire-wise, or as a component part of crests.

Pines and firs (this latter frequently found in Scottish shields) are very old symbols. A pine cone crowns the thyrse sceptre of Bacchus. It was the emblem of fertility and eternity with the Assyrians, and conveyed something of the

ARMORIAL CHIMNEY-PIECE, TATTERSHALL CASTLE.

124]

canes ; and flowered slips of the tea shrub have come to us from China and Ceylon. A branch of the tea shrub and a slip of the coffee tree, both flowered and fructed, appear in connection with the heraldic distinctions of Sir Thomas Lipton.

Laurel, or bay, is sometimes seen as small trees or bushes, but more commonly as slips or wreaths. Bayford bears : argent, a chevron between three bay leaves vert. This is, of course, a punning coat ; but branches and chaplets of bay were granted to both military and naval victors, often associated with oak leaves and acorns.

Hawthorn is generally shown as " flowered " or " fleuri," silver or red. A hawthorn bush with a crown was one of the badges of Henry VII. Sylvester bears : argent, a hawthorn tree eradicated proper. Thornholme : argent, three thorn trees vert. Thornton : argent, a chevron between three hawthorn leaves vert. Bretland : argent, a hawthorn tree eradicated vert, flowered gules.

Holly is another favourite charge in different forms. Irvine bears : argent, three holly leaves proper. Owen, co. Pembroke, bears : gules, a boar argent, armed, bristled, collared and chained or, tied to a holly bush on a mount, all proper. Foulis : argent, a holly bush between three bay leaves slipped vert. Burnet, who were hereditary Foresters to the Crown, bore the feudal Irvine coat : argent, three holly leaves or, to which they added a hunting-horn in base sable, garnished gold, stringed gules.

Willows are represented by trees, slips and osier wands. Bennison bears : argent, a willow tree vert. Count de Salis : or, a salix proper. Willis, Dean of Worcester (*obit* 1596) : argent, a chevron gules between three willow trees proper. Skirlawe, Bishop of Lichfield, Bath, and Durham (1386–1400) : argent, six osier wands interlaced in saltire (poetically described " in true love ") vert. Osier wands slipped occur in connection with the Basket Makers' Company.

Alder and ash appear chiefly for punning effect. Alderberry bears : argent, three bunches of alderberries proper. Ashton argent, an ash tree proper, issuing from a tun.

Ashford, Kent : argent, three ashen keys between two couple closes sable ; and Ashford, Cornwall : argent, a chevron between three ashen keys vert. Ashen keys are branches laden with berries.

Maple slips of three leaves are the unofficial badges of Canada, and are also found in the arms of some of the Canadian provinces. Lord Mount Stephen bore : or, on a mount, in base a maple tree proper, in chief two fleurs-de-lis azure. Both these charges are in allusion to his successful career in his adopted country, the maple of the Dominion and the blue lis of the Province of Quebec. Baron Müller, the distinguished Australian botanist, was granted : or, two branches of eucalyptus accosted, stalks interlaced, vert.

Cotton trees and branches represent textile industry. Arkwright, co. Derby, of spinning-frame celebrity, bore : argent, on a mount vert a cotton tree fructed proper ; on a chief azure between two bezants an escutcheon silver, charged with a bee volant proper. A bee volant between two fructed cotton slips is the crest of the borough of Bury, well known as a cotton-spinning centre, and its paper industry is represented by three papyrus boles in one quarter of its shield. Huddersfield has the quaint and appropriate crest of a silver ram's head couped, bearing in its mouth a cotton slip vert, fructed.

Mention of leaves has been made in connection with specific plants. But Leveson bears merely leaves for the sake of punning. A curious use of leaves is found in Germany, where crests are often borne powdered with the tender green, sweet-smelling linden leaves, or these may be placed as an ornamental fringe round the crest. When any charge is thus decorated with leaves it is said to be " verdured " or " verdoyed."

A trefoil is a leaf with three pear-shaped lobes, and is generally borne " slipped," that is to say, with a stalk. It made its appearance quite early. A Roll of Arms of Edward II's reign states that Sir Edmond de Acre bore " goules a III foiles de or, III escalops de argent." At that date " leaves " apparently was sufficient to describe the trefoil.

The shamrock, badge of St. Patrick and of Ireland, is a modification of this charge. It should be given three heart-shaped lobes and the stalk drawn wavy.

Garbs (from the French "gerbe"), or wheatsheaves, are largely used, and are found in some of the most ancient records. One of the proudest of feudal shields was that of the Earl of Chester, and we find Ranulf de Blondeville using a seal with a shield decorated with three garbs. These were blazoned in the reign of Henry III as: azure, three garbs or. One and a half of these garbs not only appear on the coat of the city of Chester, dimidiated with "England," but the sheaves were also adopted by the Hattons, Vernons, Grosvenors, Cholmondeleys and many other families of the nobility and gentry within the County Palatine of Chester, either in token of blood relationship or of feudal allegiance. Garbs also appear on the arms of the Barons Sheffield, Earls of Mulgrave, from whom they were adopted by many Yorkshire families. Garbs are often "banded" with cords of a distinct tincture. Wheat is also borne in the ear, when it may be "bearded" of a special tincture. John Wheathampstead, Abbot of St. Albans (*obit* 1464), bore: gules, a chevron between three bunches of three wheat ears each or. On the quartered coat of the town of Luton (known for its wheat straw-plaiting industry) is a wheatsheaf; and the crest is an arm, habited azure, issuing from the clouds, holding a bunch of wheat ears or. Occasionally sheaves or ears of other grain are borne, but if so the variety should be named.

Kitchen vegetables are not unrepresented. For instance, Beane bears: gules, three bean cods pendent or. Dammant: sable, a turnip leaved proper; a chief or gutty de poix. De Chauvelin, of Burgundy: argent, a cabbage eradicated vert, encircled by a serpent or. Potatoes, so far as I know, are only represented in one example, on the coat of Neuilly-sur-Seine. This town bears: gules, an arched bridge, with a ship on the waves, all argent; on a chief azure three potato flowers slipped or; the shield verdured with bunches of bulrushes and slips of potato haulms, leaved and flowered proper. Here the potato flowers are borne to commemorate the fact that Parmentier first introduced the tuber into France, planting them in the plains of Sablonville on the outskirts of Neuilly.

Nettles are sometimes classed as potherbs, and possibly Nettle, co. Cork, who bore or, a chevron gules between three nettle leaves proper, may have been of this opinion. But the allusive intent of Malherbe, co. Devon, who bore the same coat, and Mallerby, of the same county, who improved upon it by emblazoning or, a bunch of nettles vert, was decidedly derogatory. An equally unpleasant association clings to the or, three birch twigs, sable of Birtles ; the sable, a fess between two birch leaves argent, of Birche, co. Devon ; and or, three birch twigs sable, of Birches.

Other rare charges are broom, heather, mistletoe and ivy. Broom is the *planta genesta*, the celebrated badge of our Plantagenet line of kings. It is borne by Broome, co. Somerset : argent, three broom branches, vert. Brugière, Baron de Barante, Auvergne, bears : argent, a branch of heather (French *bruyère*) vert. Walbert, Normandy : or, three bars gules, over all a branch of mistletoe, vert, fructed argent. The town of St. Ives, Cornwall, has this delightful composition : a branch of green ivy spreading all over a silver shield.

Thistles, when blazoned proper, have a blue or violet flower and green leaves. This is the badge of Scotland, and was given as a mark of honour by Scottish rulers in coats of augmentation. Leven bore : argent, a thistle slipped proper ; and this, the thistle Imperially crowned, was given as a coat of augmentation to Leslie-Melville, Earls of Melville and Leven. Teasdale bears : argent, a thistle between three pheons azure ; this, evidently, in allusion to the teazle thistle.

This brings us to flowers. Certainly among the earliest and most important of these were the quatrefoils and cinquefoils, but as these are intimately linked up with the rose forms, they will be considered in connection with the Queen of Flowers in a special chapter. A large proportion of blooms known to botanists have been used, but it will only be necessary to deal with some of the most characteristic.

Lilac is represented on a French coat in the form of violet or purple quatrefoils with star-shaped piercings. That is on the shield of the pleasant Paris suburb, Les Lilas : per bend gules and azure, a bend argent charged six lilac flowers, two by two, purpure ; the shield surrounded by a branch of lilac, flowered and leaved proper. Motto : "J'etais Fleur, Je suis Cité."

LES LILAS, PARIS.

One group consists of the daisy or marguerite, the marigold, sunflower and chrysanthemum, which have a fundamentally religious significance or origin, for they are one and all representatives of the sun in glory and its fertilising powers. In the oldest symbolical renderings most of these are interchangeable and, indeed, frequently approximate to the pictorial renderings of wavy stars. As we have seen in a preceding chapter the daisy-like flowers on eleventh-century seals often merge into stars. In later heraldic representations the daisy is a pretty little flower of many white, red, or white and red petals, with a golden seed centre, and together with the marigold was adopted as a badge by many persons named Mary. It was this association that made it a favourite symbolical flower for religious bodies and persons, for they were both blooms of the Blessed Mary, and as in older systems, messengers of hope. The marigold and sunflower being flowers of Sol were also associated with gold, and were used by goldsmiths. The sunflower, shown as a huge flat seed-vessel surrounded by radiating petals, placed on a tall leaved stem, is generally borne in combination with the sun in splendour, towards which the bloom is turned, for it is the *girasole* or "heliotrope." On a seal of Margaret, daughter of Philip the Hardy, King of France, and consort of Edward I, an effigy of the queen stands, habited in a tunic "of England," with her paternal

9

and maternal arms on either side, on a corbel, the base formed
of ears of wheat and the cornice decorated with a row of marguerites.   It was also the badge of Margaret of Anjou, queen
of Henry VI, and of Margaret, Countess of Richmond, mother
of Henry VII.   This device was also used by many foreign
princesses of this name.   Daisie of Scotland bore : argent,
three daisies gules, stalked and leaved vert.   The Marquis
Marguerie (Provence): azure, three marguerites, stalked and
leaved, argent.   Pasquier (France) : or, trois marguerites
(paquerettes) d'argent, boutonné d'or.   Sunflowers being also
known as heliotropes, we find Florio bearing : azure, a
heliotrope or leaved vert, in chief a sun in splendour ; while
the Marquises d'Espaynet (Provence) bore : azure, three
marigolds on one stalk leaved or ; on a chief gules a sun in
splendour.   Within this group primroses may be included.
We find Primrose, Earls of Rosebery, bearing a truly vernal
coat : vert, three primroses within a double tressure flory
counter flory or.   Another Primrose altered the tinctures to
gold and red, quite ruining the character of the delightful
composition.   Goldman bears : gules, a chevron or between
three marigolds of the last, stalked and leaved vert.

Chrysanthemums are chiefly of interest as the sun emblems
of the East.   This flower is a constant recurring motif in
Japanese design, for it is the Imperial and national badge.
It has been conventionalised along two divergent lines : we
see it as a figure constructed on purely geometrical principles,
and also as a realistic simplification of the natural flower.
It was obviously venerated as a symbol of the sun, for the
Emperor traces his descent from the sun, Amaterasu, the
glorious daughter of Izanazi and Izanami, and this we can
see by the very treatment of the figure.   The Imperial device,
the kilku-mon, is a blossom with sixteen club-shaped petals
radiating from a circular centre, the thick portions on the
outer circumference, and a dot placed between each pair of
petals.   Its proper colours are red, with golden dots.   It is
known as the " Binding Flower," because as the bloom ties
itself together in the centre, so the Mikado binds about him
the hearts and souls of his people.   It is, in fact, the sun

JAPANESE FAMILY MONS.

1. EMPEROR'S BLAZON AND MIKADO FAMILY BLAZON.
2. BLAZON OF THE TOKUGAWA SHOGUNS BETWEEN MALLOW FLOWERS.
3. SATSUMA AND BIZEN FAMILY BLAZONS.
4. HIRATO FAMILY BLAZONS.

131

from the arms of the Cooks' Company, or Guild: argent, a chevron engrailed gules, between three columbines azure, stalked and leaved vert. Bessell bears: argent, two columbine slips crossed (in saltire) and drooping flowers purpure.

Pinks are known by the pretty old names of gilliflowers and also cloves, though the latter is misleading. They are of the single corolla type generally depicted in profile slightly conventionalised. Jollie bears: argent, three gilliflowers proper. Livingstone, Viscount Kilsyth: argent, three gilliflowers gules, pierced of the field. Cloves, the spice, are also borne. For instance, the Grocers' Guild of London has: argent, a chevron gules between nine cloves sable; Duffield; sable, a chevron between three cloves or; and Clive: or, a camel passant between three cloves sable. Violets also appear and are the floral badge of the Napoleonic dynasty. Dickens bears: argent, a chevron sable fretté or between three violets purpure, stalked and leaved vert. Pol: argent, three violets purpure, stalked sable; on a chief azure a spurrowel of eight points or.

Flowers and leaves are frequently borne in the form of wreaths, either as charges or as decorations for other charges, including human beings and beasts. Wreaths of flowers, such as of roses, are usually called chaplets. Rose chaplets are occasionally borne twined round caps, no doubt in allusion to the ancient custom of employing rose garlands on festive occasions, and with further reference to the flower symbolising among other things the duty of silence, for what was said *sub rosa* was sacred. Laurel, oak and palm wreaths are sometimes termed crowns. A figure or other charge bearing wreaths is said to be wreathed. Figures may be wreathed about the loins as well as about the head. A beast wreathed bears the chaplet about its head, but it may be gorged, or collared, with a chaplet of flowers or wreaths.

Cornucopias, or horns of plenty, are to be found as charges, as crests and as accessories to supporters. They have been employed as symbols of natural wealth and also of commerce from very remote times. They are shown brimming over with flowers and fruit. The cornucopia as a charge appears

on the arms of that popular seaside resort, Worthing, equally
known for its fisheries and its horticulture : argent, three

REPUBLIC OF PERU.

bars azure, each charged with a herring naiant ; on a chief
or a horn of plenty gules.

The term proper usually applies to tincture, but a " rose
proper gules " or " a rose proper argent " refers to the
botanical variety as distinct from the heraldic convention.
But with regard to lilies, the natural flower is most frequently
referred to as " a garden lily," or " lilies of the Virgin," to
distinguish them from the fleur-de-lis.

CHAPTER XII

MARSHALLING

MARSHALLING is the art of blending two or more coats-of-arms to form one composition, so as to convey a definite meaning.

According to modern practice the various degrees of marshalling are: the assumption of arms of dominion placed either in a shield of pretence over all, or quartered, which may be the result of conquest, inheritance or election; the adoption of feudal arms connected with fiefs, acquired either by grant, inheritance, purchase or exchange; the recording of matrimonial alliances, either by impaling, placing new arms in the shield of pretence or quartering; the assumption of arms or part of arms as the result of gifts or acceptance of directions under a will, usually associated with change of name; the use of arms attached to any particular office; the assumption of an augmentation granted by a sovereign prince.

Now let us see how this branch of the art has been evolved from very primitive forms of grouping.

Apparently the first idea connected with any change of arms resulting from conquest or the acquisition of fiefs was the substitution of the arms appertaining to the new property for the paternal arms. This was done even by knights who married heiresses. And there are records where the holder of a fief agreed to sell it, together with all rights in his feudal arms. But the more usual way was to group a set of shields on seals, surcoats and horse caparisons, an arrangement specially rife in the thirteenth century. On seals we see three shields grouped in triangle, four or five in cross; at other times one shield or more may hang from a tree; or we

IMPALED COATS (DURHAM GUILDS).

136]

have the effigy of the owner in armorial surcoat or robe, holding one shield or more. Sometimes we may have the paternal shield surrounded by crests, badges or charges from other arms. For, as Wyrley says in his " True Use of Arms," " divers did add unto the mark of their own house some part of the device of the family from which their mothers descended," even " some part of the device of him who advanced them." On surcoats we may find the chief coat on chest and back, with different bearings on the ailerons or short sleeves. Much the same practice was adopted with horse caparisons, the covering of the body having the chief bearings, that of the neck other arms.

Reverting to seals, we find the arms of the husband on the seal, and that of the wife on the counter seal. Ela, Countess of Warwick (*circa* 1240), daughter of William Longespée, Earl of Salisbury, on her widowhood married Philip Basset. All this is recorded quite plainly on her seal, for we find her effigy bearing in her dexter hand a shield of the arms of Longespée, in her left a shield of the arms of Newburgh, Earl of Warwick, while on the counter seal are the arms of Basset. Sometimes the effigy stands between shields charged respectively with the husband's and the paternal bearings. Another daughter of Longespée married a knight of the name of Audele, and their son, Sir James Audele, bore over his paternal arms a label azure, with a lion rampant or on each point, to denote his maternal descent. Instances of this method are numerous. The seal of Margaret Logie, second wife of David II of Scotland, is placed between three shields : Scotland, Logie (her first husband) and Drummond (paternal). Another interesting seal is that of Elizabeth de Clare, daughter and heiress of Gilbert de Clare, Earl of Gloucester, a niece of Edward II. She was a much married *grande dame*. The central shield is that of Roger d'Amori, the third husband, which is surrounded by three lions passant-guardant of England to show her royal descent. A cross of tracery embraces four armorial shields, the upper one being that of John de Burgh, Earl of Ulster, her first husband ; in base we see the fret of Theobald de Verdon, her second husband ; and on either side are the arms of Clare. In the four angles are trefoil compartments, two containing castles, and two having lions rampant, these being borne in allusion to her grandmother, Eleanor of Castile and Leon, wife of Edward I. We see this system also on the royal seals. On the Great Seal of Edward II, the King's effigy is flanked by two hexagonal castles representing his descent from Eleanor of Castile ; and on the second Great Seal of Edward III, we find fleurs-de-lis placed close to his throne, which refer to his mother. Robert de Clifford bore : chequy or and azure, a fess gules, and on his seal attached to the Barons' letter to the Pope (1301), the shield is surrounded by annulets, which he derived from his mother, Isabel, daughter and co-heiress of Robert de Vipont, who bore : or, six annulets gules. John de Dreux, Earl of Richmond, son of John, Duke of Brittany, and Beatrice Plantagenet, second daughter of Henry III (born 1266), bore : chequy or and azure (for Dreux), a canton ermine (for Brittany, an heiress of that House having been married), surrounded by a border of England, *i.e.*, gules, charged with lions passant-guardant or, to record his descent from Beatrice and Henry III. Both the canton and the border were constantly used for this purpose. John of Eltham, second son of Edward II and his queen Isabel of France, differenced his royal arms of England with a border of France.

Mention of the label for the same purpose has already been made in connection with the de Longespée descent. Other famous examples may be adduced. Edmond Crouchback, Earl of Lancaster, second son of Henry III, after his marriage with Blanche, daughter of Robert, Comte d'Artois, bore : England differenced with a label of France, *i.e.*, azure a fleur-de-lis or, on each point. His grandson, Henry Plantagenet, first Duke of Lancaster, bore the same label. Edmond in this matter followed the example of his father-in-law, for Robert d'Artois, brother of St. Louis, bore France ancient differenced by a label of Castile (gules, a castle or on each point). Lionel, Duke of Clarence, Earl of Ulster, third son of Edward III, after his marriage with Elizabeth de Burgh, who as heiress of her father brought him the Earldom, bore a label with the red crosses of Ulster. Sir John Bourchier, Baron Berners (*circa* 1475), bore a label of England, each of the points being charged with three gold lions, in allusion to his mother, Anne, daughter of Thomas, Duke of Gloucester, sixth son of Edward III. His brother, William Bourchier, Lord Fitzwarren, bore a label of France.

A curious use of the label to denote descent, where the paternal arms had been abandoned in favour of a feudal coat, occurs in connection with Charlton of Powys, who bears Powys: or, a lion rampant gules, with a label vert, on each point an eagle or; the old arms of Charlton being: vert, three eagles or. This was a change resulting from succession to what amounted to a fief. A similar abandonment of paternal arms and the assumption of specially marshalled arms of dominion is seen in the case of Richard, Emperor of Germany ("King of the Romans"), Earl of Poitou and Cornwall, son of King John. The arms of Poitou are: argent, a lion rampant gules, crowned or; those of Cornwall: sable, bezantée. So he bore the arms of Poitou within a border of Cornwall. His son Edmond placed his shield over an Imperial eagle, the shield being suspended from the guige held in the supporter's beak. Richard's natural son, Richard of Cornwall, bore the same arms, but had the border engrailed. His successor, Sir Geoffrey de Cornwall, having taken the Duke of Brittany prisoner, changed his field to ermine; the Brittany arms being ermine plain. We find the same thing happening in France. Hugo, third son of Henry I of France, Earl of Vermandois by marriage with an heiress whose county he thus acquired, abandoned the lilies for: chequy or and azure. Robert, fourth son of Louis le Gros, Earl of Dreux, also changed his lilies for the chequy or and azure of Dreux. Pierre, fifth son of Louis, having married the heiress of the House of Courtney substituted their three torteaux for his fleurs-de-lis. According to the metrical historian of the Siege of Carlaverock Sir Nicholas de Segrave bore a lion sable, his father having discarded his ancient sheaves of corn. Now, it is found, by the seal of John de Segrave attached to the either by impaling or by quartering, place their charges (and more particularly animated charges) " contourné," so as to face each other. It is a peculiarity that has to be carefully borne in mind, as it may be misleading.

Marshalling of augmentations offers some peculiarity and opens up a wide field full of interest. Augmentations are additions made to existing arms by sovereign princes by way of reward or compliment. They may take the form of a charge or a complete composition. In the latter case they may be borne in an escutcheon of pretence, on a chief, a canton or even a bend. As regards charges, our own kings have granted lions of England, roses (of York, of Lancaster and Tudor) and fleurs-de-lis ; the Scottish kings were lavish with the double bordure flory counter flory, especially to record family alliances, and have also granted thistles ; the French kings bestowed the fleurs-de-lis ; the Emperors the Imperial and also the Apostolic eagles. In later time Napoleon I bestowed his Imperial bees and eagles, and the Cross of the Legion of Honour, the last course also being adopted by his nephew ; while the Emperor of Germany has bestowed the Iron Cross of Valour. Among famous single charges are the red heart of Bruce, long borne crowned by the Douglas family ; the blue sword borne palewise supporting a royal crown, seen on the shield of Setons, and granted to Sir Alexander Seton for his defence of Berwick about 1320 ; the arms of Scotland, but with a demi lion vulned in the mouth by an arrow, granted to Thomas Howard, Duke of Norfolk, by Henry VIII, to commemorate his victory at Flodden Field and the slaying of James IV. To Sir John Clerk for his capture of the Duc de Longueville at the Battle of the Spurs, Henry VIII granted : on a canton azure a demi ram saliant argent, armed or, in chief two fleurs-de-lis gold, over all a baton of the second. The Duke was a grandson of Jean, Duc d'Orleans, and he bore France differenced with a label, and a ram for crest. Of a different nature were the grants made by Richard II. Not only did he himself assume the mythical arms of Edward the Confessor, bearing them impaled with his own, but he bestowed them on his kinsmen

QUARTERED AND IMPALED COAT.

the Hollands, Dukes of Surrey and Kent, and also on Thomas Mowbray, Duke of Norfolk, who quartered them with their paternal arms. Richard also gave to Robert de Vere, whom he created Duke of Ireland, the mythical arms of St. Edmund, which about that time became regarded as the insignia of the sister isle. In the same order of affairs Henry VIII granted to Thomas Manners, Earl of Rutland, in token of his descent from Anne Plantagenet, a chief quarterly of France and England, which the Dukes still bear. He also made grants of elaborate augmentations to most of his wives, as described in Chapter XXIV, which, however, contain very confused and misleading ideas of alliance.

With us the eighteenth and nineteenth centuries were prolific in military and naval augmentations. Nelson was granted a chief wavy azure, waves of the sea, from which a palm tree issues between a disabled ship on the dexter and a ruined battery on the sinister. Admiral Duncan, for his victory of Camperdown, had to remove his family chevron to make room for a representative of a medal of honour presented to him by the King, together with the word " Camperdown." Lord Hawke, for his victory over the French fleet, 1759, was awarded : argent, a chevron ermine between three boatswains' whistles, erect, proper. Supporters, dexter, Neptune with a trident, standing on a dolphin ; sinister, a seahorse holding a flag staff with Union Jack in its paws. The Duke of Marlborough received a chief : argent, a cross of St. George, thereon an escutcheon of the arms of France. That granted to General Gerald Lake, created Baron Lake by George III, for his victory over the Maharatas, is curious as taking us back to ancient symbolism. He bears on a silver chief the fish of the Mogul Emperors, per pale or and vert, banded vert and gules, surmounting the Goog and Ullum in saltire. This is the Mahi Maratib, a golden carp, partly enveloped in a mantle of green brocade, the badge of the kings of Oudhe, placed over their wands of office. The Duke of Wellington was granted the Union badge (Union Jack) to be borne on a shield in the honour point.

10

More peaceful in character was the grant made to the father of Captain John Speke, in recognition of his dead son's exploration of the Nile.   On a chief is a river with the word " Nile."   The crest is a crocodile, and the supporters a crocodile and a hippopotamus.

CHAPTER XIII

DIFFERENCING AND MARKS OF CADENCY

DIFFERENCING practically forms a branch of Marshalling. It is the art of introducing certain variations in armorial bearings with a view to give individuality to the shields of each member, or group of members, of a family, without losing the main characteristics which unite them all. This, of course, includes the modern system of recording cadency by the introduction of small charges on the shields of each son. These are called Marks of Cadency, which are assigned as follows : a label to the eldest son, a crescent to the second son, mullet to the third son, martlet fourth, annulet fifth, fleur-de-lis sixth, rose seventh, cross moline eighth, double quatrefoil ninth. These are generally placed on the honour point of the shield, and should also be borne on the crest and badge, if any. These marks of cadency may themselves be charged. Thus the eldest son of a second son would charge his father's crescent with a label, and so on. If we adhered strictly to this system, such differencing should go on indefinitely, either until older branches die out or some permanent difference, such as the introduction of additional charges, or quartering, produce new bearings. It must be confessed, however, that the use of marks of cadency is not observed with any degree of precision with us, and our system is not recognised in its entirety by authorities abroad.

Before the fifteenth century great diversity was shown in methods of differencing. Of our present-day marks of cadency practically only the label received general recogthree hurts; Sir Richard, Earl of Salisbury, eldest son by the second marriage, a label gobony argent and azure, this being derived from his mother, a Beaufort, who bore the royal arms within a border gobony of those tinctures.   George, Lord Latimer, placed an ogress, or possibly an annulet, on his saltire ; Robert, Bishop of Durham, used two annulets interlaced; William, Lord Fauconberg, Earl of Kent, a mullet ; Edward, Lord Abergavenny, a rose, possibly in allusion to his mother's royal Lancastrian descent.   Others of the family used fleurs-de-lis and cinquefoils. A remarkable heraldic arrangement is that of the Zouches in the fourteenth century. Alan le Zouche, head of the family, bore : gules, bezanté. On his seal his shield hangs from the neck of a demi lion and is surrounded by six lions, to show his descent from Ela, daughter and co-heiress of Stephen de Longespée, who bore six lions rampant. His nearest cousin, William le Zouche of Haryngworth, charged the shield with a quarter ermine ; William, of Leicestershire, a label azure; Oliver, a chevron ermine ; Amory, a bend argent ; Thomas, on a quarter argent, a mullet sable.

Another fine series is connected with the Cobham's gules, a chevron or—younger members placing on the chevron three mullets, three lions, three cross-crosslets, three fleurs-de-lis, three crescents, and three martlets, in every case of sable hue.

A very good example of modern difference, conceived in the best heraldic tradition, is seen in the arms of Colonel du Pré Penton Powney : sable, a fess cotised and couped argent, between five mascles, four in chief and one in base, also silver. He derives through the distaff side from the Powneys of Old Windsor, who bore : sable, a fess argent in chief three mascles of the last. For crest, a demi eagle displayed charged on the breast with a mascle argent.

As regards the introduction of ordinaries or sub-ordinaries, the border was long the favourite with younger members of our royal family. Edmund, Earl of Kent, younger son of Edward I, bore England within a border argent. Thomas of Woodstock, Duke of Gloucester, youngest son of Edward III, bore France and England quarterly within a border argent.

Humphrey, Duke of Gloucester, youngest son of Henry IV, bore the same quarterings, first within a border of gobony argent and sable, and then within a plain border of argent. John Plantagenet, Earl of Kent, second son of Edmond of Woodstock, sixth son of Edward I, bore England within a border argent. Richard, Earl of Cambridge, grandson of Edward III, England within a border argent charged with ten lions rampant gules. Then we have the famous Beaufort difference. John and Henry Beaufort, sons of John of Gaunt and Catherine, widow of Sir Otes Swinford, after their legitimation, placed the royal arms within a border gobony argent and azure. Thomas Beaufort, Duke of Exeter, the third son, had his border at first of azure and ermine, but, after his creation as Duke, altered it to gobony argent and azure semée of fleurs-de-lis. Thomas Holland, Earl of Kent, son of Thomas Holland and Joan Plantagenet, Fair Maid of Kent, was granted by his half-brother Richard II, the arms of England within a border argent. His brother John Holland had a border of France, as did the third son of Henry. The border, plain or charged, was largely used in noble families of the west of England and Scotland for the same purpose. While de Vere, Earl of Oxford (1266), bore : quarterly, gules and or, a mullet in the first quarter, his brother differenced with a border indented sable. The Lyon Register of Scotland introduced a regular system whereby the first cadets had a plain border of the tincture of the principal charge ; other cadets had the border engrailed, invected, etc. ; while the third generation had theirs charged ; and with the fourth the border was divided per pale, per fess, or quarterly. The border wavy and engrailed was unfortunately adopted as a mark of illegitimacy. So that while we find Walter Stewart, son by the second marriage of Robert II, bearing (1389) Scotland within a border chequy argent and azure, we also see the illegitimate Douglas of Drumlanrig, and the Stewarts, Earls of Lennox, differencing with engrailed borders.

Just before the marriage of Princess Victoria of Battenberg to the King of Spain, a warrant was issued assigning her the arms of her father : quarterly, first and fourth azure, a lion rampant double queué, barry of ten gules and argent, crowned, and holding in the right paw a sword proper (for Hesse), within a border gobony of sixteen pieces of the third and second ; second and third, argent, two mullets sable (for Battenberg), the whole within a border of England, the supporters carrying banners of the royal arms of England.

Abroad the border was also largely used to difference the bearings of younger members of royal houses, in Spain and Portugal, these being charged so as to show maternal descent. Philip of France, Duke of Burgundy, bore France within a border gobony and gules.

Chevrons were introduced into their arms by younger members of French families, the same thing taking place in Scotland and occasionally in England. The canton was essentially the mark of cadency in the Low Countries and was sometimes used by us for the same purpose, having the advantage of being treated like a subsidiary shield whereon descent or alliance can be shown. In France the Bourbons, in addition to the border, showed a predilection for bends of different kinds. The Dukes of Bourbon used for brisure a bend cotised gules ; the Dukes of Montpensier, a bend gules, the upper part charged with the cross of the Dauphiné; the Prince of Condé, a baton couped in bend ; the Princess of Conti followed suit, but added a border gules ; the Counts d'Estampes, France ancient differenced by a bend gobony gules and ermine ; the Counts of Evreux, a bend gobony argent and gules ; the Bourbons of la Roche sur Yon, France modern, a cotice in bend gules, charged with a silver crescent in chief.

Several instances of changes of tincture have already been given. This was the method adopted by the Balliols (temp. Henry III). The Berkeleys originally bore gules, a chevron or ; but the chevron is also found changed to silver, and for further distinction other members added crosses patée and roses both argent, and the branch in Leicestershire, cinquefoils. In France we find Bourbers-Abbeville-Tunc bearing : argent, three inescutcheons gules ; while Abbeville-Bourbers-Tunc bore : or, three inescutcheons gules.

As to powdering the field, we find this done by Sir Edmond

BOOK PLATE OF COLONEL DU PRÉ PENTON POWNEY.

Dacre of Westmorland (*temp*. Edward II), who, to difference his shield from that borne by the head of the family gules, three escallop shells or, added a powder of golden trefoils.

Coming to the problem of differencing for illegitimacy it must be remembered that, however hard the law treated bastardy, in the social life of the Middle Ages and even long after, little distinction was made as regards birth, of course apart from questions of inheritance. Bastards filled important offices, intermarried with the legitimate issue of great houses, and so, provided both parents were of gentle blood, no difficulty was made about their bearing armorial shields. Only these had to be clearly differenced, and from earliest days the bend sinister, or preferably its diminutive the bendlet sinister, was that mark. This seemed quite appropriate, for it came from the " coté femme " of the shield, drawing a debruising mark right across the field. This mark of bastardy is mentioned in various Ordinances of different countries. But the regulations were never strictly observed. Soon, indeed, the bendlet was couped at both ends, and so we have what the French call the " baton perri en barre," whence have come the popular but erroneous phrases of " bastard bar " and "bar sinister." Another modification was soon introduced. In order to make the debruising less conspicuous the bendlet sinister was frequently carried under and not over any ordinary used as a charge.

The use of the bend sinister for debruising suggested another system of marshalling, that of placing the paternal arms on an ordinary, such as a bend, a fess, a chevron or a canton. The Beauforts, sons of John of Gaunt and Catherine Swinford, before the legitimation by Parliament, bore the arms of their father (gules, three lions passant-guardant, or, differenced with a label of three points ermine) on a bend, placed on a shield per pale argent and azure. Sir Roger de Clarendon, the reputed illegitimate son of the Black Prince, marshalled his father's " shield of peace " arranged on a bend, bearing : argent, on a bend sable three ostrich feathers bendwise, enfiled with a scroll argent. The same practice was adopted abroad. It was done by Mathieu, Baron de la Roche, le

Grand Batard de Bourbon, who bore a bend of France, debruised by a cotice gules, on a silver shield. Antoine, Comte de la Roche, le Grand Batard de Bourgogne, did the same with his quartered coat, the field being gold. The fess was used for displaying his arms by Charles Somerset, eldest son of Charles Somerset, Earl of Worcester, bastard son of Henry Beaufort, third Duke of Somerset, but the practice was soon abandoned, and his present-day descendants use the coat of the legitimate Beauforts. The fess arrangement was adopted by Jean, Batard de Bourgogne, Bishop of Cambray (*obit* 1479); while Philippe, Batard de Bourgogne, seigneur de Fontaines, illegitimate son of a legitimate son of Antoine, " le grand Batard," marshalled his quartered coat in a chevron placed on a gold shield.

Most of the illegitimate offspring of the English and British kings debruised their arms with bends or bendlets sinister, but there were other exceptions besides the Beauforts. Sir John de Clarence, natural son of Thomas, Duke of Clarence, son of Henry IV, bore : per chevron gules and azure, in chief two lions counter-rampant regardant, in base a fleur-de-lis or. While we have here the royal charges, the composition produces something quite new. Henry Fitzroy, Duke of Richmond and Somerset, natural son of Henry VIII, was granted : the royal arms within a border quarterly ermine and counter gobony or and azure, debruised by a baton sinister argent ; over all an escutcheon of pretence : quarterly, gules and vaire or and vert, a lion rampant, argent, on a chief azure a castle between two bucks' heads silver, attired gold. It is impossible to say what this escutcheon may have been intended to convey, but it is on a level with the muddled heraldry of the king's many wives. Another unusual marshalling was that of James Fitzroy, Duke of Monmouth, natural son of Charles II : quarterly, first and fourth, ermine on a pile gules three lions of England ; second and third, or, a shield of France within the royal tressure of Scotland. This, however, was soon abandoned for the royal arms debruised with a bendlet sinister, and with a shield of pretence of Scott of Buccleuch.

Apart from the natural children of royalty, the bendlet

sinister, or its diminutive the baton sinister, was practically disused in England after the sixteenth century, when borders, often wavy, were substituted. Even these mild reminders have frequently been dropped after a few generations.

List of Royal Labels

Geoffrey Plantagenet, Earl of Brittany and Richmond, fourth son of Henry II (1158–1186), a label of five points.

Edward I, as heir apparent, a label of five points azure; also one of three points. This label was also borne by Edward II and Edward III when heirs apparent. But Edward the Black Prince used a silver label of three points, and ever since his time this has been the label of the Princes of Wales.

Edmond, Earl of Lancaster, second son of King Henry III, a label of three points charged with nine fleurs-de-lis; also a label of three points azure with three fleurs-de-lis on each point or. His son, Thomas, bore the same label. All his descendants seem to have differenced alike.

Lionel, Duke of Clarence, Earl of Ulster, third son of Edward III, a label of three points argent, each charged with a canton gules.

John of Gaunt, Duke of Lancaster, King of Castile and Leon, third son of Edward III, a label of three points ermine. His son Henry, before his accession to the throne, a label of five points, the three to the dexter ermine, and the two to the sinister azure, with three fleurs-de-lis on each point.

Edmond, Duke of York, fifth son of Edward III, a label of three points argent, on each point three torteaux.

Thomas of Lancaster, Duke of Clarence, son of Henry IV, a label of three points ermine, each charged with a canton gules.

John, Duke of Bedford, third son of Henry IV, a label of five points, the two to the dexter ermine, the other three azure with three fleurs-de-lis.

Edward, Duke of York, eldest son of Edmond of Langley, a label of three points gules, on each as many castles or.

Richard II, during the lifetime of his father, a label of three points argent, the centre charged with a cross of St. George.

Richard, Earl of Cambridge, second son of Edmond of Langley (and grandson of Edward III), a label of three points each charged with as many torteaux.

Richard, Duke of York, son of the above, the same label.

Edmond, of York, Earl of March, third son of Richard, Duke of York, a label of five points argent, the two dexter points charged with as many lions rampant purpure, and the three sinister with nine torteaux.

Richard, Duke of York, second son of Edward IV, a label of three points argent, charged with a canton gules, which was also borne by the sixth son, George, Duke of Clarence; while the Duke of Clarence's son, Edward, Earl of Warwick, bore a label of three points gobony argent and azure.

Arthur Tudor, Prince of Wales, eldest son of Henry VII, a label of three points argent.

James, Duke of York, third son of Charles I, a label of three points ermine.

Henry, Duke of Gloucester, fourth son of Charles I, a label of three points argent, each charged with a rose gules.

George III. The sons bore their labels differenced as follows:

Duke of York, Bishop of Osnaburgh, cross of St. George in the centre point.

William Henry, Duke of Clarence (subsequently King William IV), a cross of St. George between two anchors gules.

Edward, Duke of Kent, a cross of St. George between fleurs-de-lis gules.

Ernest Augustus, Duke of Cumberland, a fleur-de-lis gules between two crosses of St. George. His son the second Duke, a label of three points gules, the centre point charged with the white horse of Hanover.

Augustus Frederick, Duke of Sussex, two hearts on centre point gules and a cross of St. George on the outer points.

Adolphus Frederick, Duke of Cambridge, a cross of St. George on the middle and two red hearts on each of the outer points. This label was borne by his son George, the second Duke, who placed immediately beneath it a label of five points gules.

Duke of Gloucester, a label of five points, on centre point a fleur-de-lis between a cross of St. George on the outer points. His son, the second Duke, had a label of five points, the centre one having a fleur-de-lis, and the four outer points crosses of St. George.

Charlotte Augustus, Princess Royal, Queen of Wurtemberg, a rose between two crosses of St. George. Her husband, the Prince of Saxe-Coburg, a label of five points, a red rose on the centre point.

Princess Augusta Sophia, a rose between two ermine spots.

Princess Elizabeth, Princess of Hesse, a cross of St. George between two roses gules.

Princess Mary, a rose between two cantons.

Princess Sophia, a heart between two roses.

Princess Amelie, a rose between two hearts.

Queen Victoria's children were all assigned silver labels of three points with the following charges: Alfred, Duke of Edinburgh, a cross of St. George on the central point and a red anchor on each of the outer points. His son, Duke of Saxe-Coburg-Gotha, a cross of St. George between two hearts. Arthur, Duke of Connaught, a cross of St. George and two red fleurs-de-lis. Prince Arthur of Connaught, a label of five points argent, the centre and outer points charged with a cross of St. George and the others with a fleur-de-lis azure. Leopold, Duke of Albany, a cross of St. George and two red hearts. Victoria, Princess Royal of England, Empress of Germany, a red rose and two crosses of St. George. Princess Alice of Hesse, a red rose and two ermine spots. Helena, Princess Christian, a cross of St. George and two red roses. Louise, Duchess of Argyll, a red rose and two red cantons. Beatrice, Princess Henry of Battenberg, a red heart and two red roses.

King Edward's daughters, granted while their father was Prince of Wales:

Princess Louise, Princess Royal, Duchess of Fife, a label of five points, the middle and outer points charged with a cross of St. George, the others with a thistle, slipped and leaved.

Princess Victoria, five points, the centre and outer points charged with a rose gules, the others with a cross of St. George.

Princess Maud, Queen of Norway, five points, the centre and outer points being a red heart, the others a cross of St. George.

CHAPTER XIV

CANTING ARMS

A REMARKABLE feature of heraldry, not only English, but of all countries, consists of what the French call "*armes parlantes*." These "speaking arms" we describe technically as "allusive" or as "canting arms," the latter a term derived from chanting, to sing out, and are so called because they enable even the uninitiated to connect the coat-of-arms, crest and badge with its owner. They are, in other words, pictorial puns. This form of blazoning is very old. Some of the earliest examples of the twelfth and thirteenth centuries belong to this class. It served a useful purpose in its day, for it made the "cognisance" specially recognisable to both gentle and simple folk in the traffickings of peace and in time of war. But even in this direction we find warrant for the practice in quite remote days. Probably the heroes of antiquity began it on their metal or leather shields. Certainly Plutarch gives an instance of early emblematic punning. He tells us that when Cicero went as quæstor to Sicily, " he consecrated in one of the temples a vase, or some other offering in silver, upon which he inscribed his two first names, Marcus Tullius, and, punning upon the third, ordered the artificer to engrave a ' vetch.' " As we all know, Cicero was an inveterate punster, a weakness which caused him to commit many crimes against good taste and kindly fellowship. But his example was largely followed, emblematically as well as verbally.

In an old Herald's " Visitation Book," covering only a small part of England, of 1240–1245, we find no less than nine examples of these "speaking arms." It is somewhat curious

to note, on the study of other Herald's " Visitation Books "
and armorial dictionaries, that this peculiar form of human
weakness was rather more widely prevalent in the North
than in the South of England. Whether this was due to the
slower spread of clerkly learning, or to the more steadfast
clinging to feudal customs, it is hard to say ; but later it
became a mannerism, fostered, no doubt, by the lamentable
proneness of man to give way to evil habits. One is the more
induced to think this because of the shockingly bad work of
some of the pictorial punsters. It is true that this is the
reflection of a twentieth-century critic on the work of those
of other ages and modes of thought and speech. Indeed, we
find that some of those " speaking arms " are practically dumb
to us, because we have re-christened many things and altered
our phonetics. Thus, the family of Skenes bear three dirks
(anciently skenes) ; the Lucies of olden fame, three fishes
which turn out to be pikes, better known to our ancestors
by the more poetic name of lucies. Our " fishy " friends
are numerous. On the very old shield of the Comtes de
Bar, who were so intimately connected with our Plantagenet kings, were two barbels (French, *barres*) embowed.
Almost of equal age, the Troutbecks have a charming arrangement of mountain trout. The Turbuts have three turbots,
the Whalleys can boast of three whales, and the Salmons three
salmons. That once formidable man, Peter des Roches,
Bishop of Winchester, had three roaches. This is curious,
because the Norman name appears to be derived from *roche*,
a rock, upon which their seigneurial castle was built. In
fact, that grand bishop was named Stone Rock, his god-
parents being as guilty of tautology as the civic wags of
Margate, who talk of Cliftonville. Argent, three eels naiant,
azure, are the arms of Eeles. Then we have the following :
Spratt : argent, a chevron sable between three sprats azure.
Sturgeon : azure; three sturgeons naiant, argent. Mackerel :
gules, three mackerel hauriant, argent. De Soles : gules,
three soles argent. Robert, Lord Scales (*circa* 1300), descendant of Eschales of Lynn, Norfolk, bore : gules, six escallop
shells argent. Sable, a fess engrailed between three whelk

shells, stood for Shelley. Atsea bore: or, two bars wavy, gules, between three shrimps of the second; and Sea: argent, a fish hauriant, azure, between two of the second, each charged with as many bars nebulé of the first; for crest: two lobster claws erect gule, each clutching a fish argent.

Among the obsolete puns perhaps the arms of the Trusbuts, Barons of Wartre, should be included. They bore "trois boutz d'eau," or three water bowgets, those skins of animals used by the Crusaders for storing water—and sometimes for stronger liquids. In this instance the punster endeavoured to kill two birds at one " go," having a shy at the family name and baronial title with the three water bags.

Fruits, flowers, and plants are largely drawn upon, as we have already seen. Other examples are afforded. Pawne bore: argent, three peacocks in their pride proper, evidently in allusion to the French word *paon*. The far-spread Fraser family bear: azure, three frases, that is, strawberry flowers, from the French *fraisier*. Primrose bears: or, three primroses within a double tressure flory, counter flory gules. Azure, three lilies argent, stood for Lillie, and also for Beauty, whose appreciation of what is really beautiful and sense of humour are to be commended. Periton bears: or, a pear-tree vert, fructed proper; and Warden: argent, three warden pears leaved vert. Argent, a fess sable, between three apples, gules, stalked vert, are the arms of the Appletons, of Surrey. By the way, it may perhaps be as well to state that every " mother's son " of us is fully entitled to the apple as an heraldic personal cognisance: that is, if we may believe the celebrated French herald Freron. This worthy sage declares that Adam after the fall adopted a fig leaf as his armorial insignia and that Abel and the rest of his progeny quartered the paternal arms with those of Mother Eve, who was an heiress, and bore: argent, an apple vert. Clearly then these arms are ours. But to return to our proper subject.

In the chapter dealing with animals in heraldry a varied array of punning coats has been given, but a few more instances may be mentioned here. Thomas Ramridge,

II

crest, emblazoned it thrice over on his shield and then, in the course of time, the Von Steins became Falconsteins. Sceptics may, of course, doubt the legend from beginning to end, but the fact that Steins preceded the Falconsteins in the Black Forest is beyond dispute, and also that the former bore a plain shield with a cross, and the latter bear falcons.

Even greater freedom was given to fancy when designing the personal badge and the rebus. Sir John Peché (early sixteenth century) used for his badge a peach slipped argent, charged with the letter E. A fructed peach branch was his crest, and he surrounded his arms with a beautiful wreath of peach leaves and fruit, each fruit bearing the letter E. Markham had a lion of St. Mark, its wings displayed, supporting a horse collar (hames). Sir Godfrey Foljambe, of Walton, Derby, had as one of his badges a human leg couped at the thigh, vestured per pale or and sable, spurred or. Catesby's golden leopard passant was probably intended for a cat o' mountain passing by. Ashton had an ash growing out of a tun, and Burton a bird standing on one. Bishop Thomas Beckington's rebus was a fire-beacon, a tun and the letter T. Oldham, that busy Lancashire town, used owls as supporters for its civic arms ; and it is curious to find Oldham, Bishop of Exeter, adopting an owl bearing in its beak a scroll with the word Dom. Abbot Ramridge, whose arms have already been noticed, also sported a badge, consisting of a ram with a collar bearing the word " Ryge." Abbot Islip's chapel at Westminster Abbey shows two different versions of his rebus. The first represents a man falling from a tree, and exclaiming " I slip." In the second instance we have a human eye and a branch or slip from a tree. The Oxenbridge Chapel in St. George's, Windsor Castle, has sculptured over the doorway the founder's badge—an ox, a capital N, and a bridge. In St. Albans Abbey Church John Wheathamstede has a cluster of wheat ears between an eagle and a Paschal lamb, the symbols of St. John the Evangelist and St. John the Baptist. In Canterbury Cathedral the eagle, standing over an ox branded with the letters, N E, stands for John Oxney.

CHAPTER XV

THE FLEUR-DE-LIS AND ITS VARIATIONS

CERTAIN decorative forms seem to spring naturally from the human mind. This does not solely apply to the strictly geometrical figures. It is equally true as regards such conventionalised emblems as the cross with expanded limbs (the so-called cross patée, or more correctly formée, of the heralds), the tau and the ansata crosses, which we find in Egyptian, Eastern, and in Central American memorial carvings, some of which belong to periods long anterior to the dawn of our own era, in certain instances occurring spontaneously in each region. An example of this also appears to exist in the Fleur-de-lis.

In Europe from mediæval times downwards force of circumstance has conspired to endow the beautiful figure with a peculiarly French character. The French themselves say that they owe their lilies to Clovis, and it is worth noting that according to a very old legend they were a gift direct from heaven to the first Christian king of the Franks, they having been brought by an angel to a pious hermit for transmission to the monarch. This in itself is evidence of the extreme antiquity of these emblems, an antiquity which shrouded their beginning in obscurity. It is true that opponents of the miraculous have assigned amusingly divergent theories as to this origin. Botanists look upon it as the arbitrary form of the iris, supposed to have been used as a primitive sceptre for early chieftains ; others think it is the riverside flag, the yellow flowers of which were plucked by the victorious soldiers of Clovis after the battle of Tolbiac to adorn their flowing locks, and so adopted as a royal badge. We are also told that it may be a painter's rendering of the bee, very doubt-fully asserted to have been the badge of Childeric ; or even the three frogs which foreigners attributed to the Gauls. But the two great opposing schools are those who believe the emblem represents the garden lily, the white lily of the Virgin Mary ; and those who, with some show of reason, regard it

FRANCE ANCIENT.

as a war symbol, a beauti-ful partisan or pike head. If we consult old documents and monuments, evidence may be found to support each of these theories, and several more. Deeper study, however, can lead to but one conclusion, and that is, the fleur-de-lis is a conven-tionalised marsh or water flower. Its prototype may have been yellow blossom of the river flags, or the charm-ing iris (which, by a natural transition, would be over-laid with gold, for " painting the rose and gilding refined gold " has ever been a favourite pastime), or, again, it may have been the Eastern lotus. Egyptians and Asiatics held the lotus sacred, not only as a food-giving plant, but as a symbol of fertility, the product of earth and water vivified by solar heat, exhibiting the striking phenomena of opening and shutting with the rise and setting of the sun. Hence it was sacred to Phthah, to Osiris and Isis, all relating to the Nile and its wondrous floods. In the East, Vishnu issues from the floating lotus, symbolising the creation of the world from chaos. Possibly this lotus may have travelled westward through Greece and Rome. On the other hand, it belongs to the common fund of symbolism, and while the nenupha spoke of the life-giving overflowing Nile to the dwellers in Egypt, the lotus pictured fertility to the Hindus, the iris and kindred growths budding luxuriantly on the

river bank foreshadowed spring to others. It is certain that
we find the Greeks and Etruscans using a fleur-de-lis, and
generally in much the same sense as the Egyptians did the
lotus—as a sign of plenty and happiness. In this sense, too,
was it employed by the Romans on some of their coins and
medals—the French say chiefly in connection with Gaul.
It is notable enough that many of the numismatic horns of
plenty have a trifolated object in the mouth of the cornucopia,
and this occurs on coins struck in Rome as well as in the
distant provinces.

The fleur-de-lis belongs to the mystic triparted symbols
so early venerated. In later times, like the shamrock, it
told the devout of the Blessed Trinity ; while still later heralds
saw in it a painted sermon, silently appealing to knights and
squires, the three lobes standing for " Sapience, foy et
prouesse." Finally the politically minded declared that the
three lobes, and the three flowers on the royal shield,
referred to the three early races of French kings.

One difficulty in treating this subject is that in spite of
the great diversity of shapes given to the fleur-de-lis—though
throughout its primal character is maintained—it is practically impossible to assign dates to these different varieties,
as they are used simultaneously, especially so in the early
days. For instance, we find a perfect conventionalised
fleur-de-lis in the ancient hieroglyphics of Upper Egypt. In
the Zodiac room of the temple of Denderah were to be seen
three floral sceptres—one is topped by a bell-shaped flower,
a mere outline of the symbolical lotus ; a second has a calyx
formed of two sepals, with an inner lanceolate bud ; the
third has at the top two steps, from the smaller of which
springs an exact fleur-de-lis of the strictest Bourbon period.
Perrot and Chipiez give a picture of a fleur-de-lis from a
gem of the Mycenæan period. It is of the iris type, having a
central oval petal, two curving outward petals, with ball
anthers, a fillet, but no stalk.

A complete fleur-de-lis consists of three petals, a transverse
fillet, and beneath this the stalk. Sometimes filaments are
placed between the central petal and outer curved ones,

In one type we find the two curved outer petals joined together and forming a cup or calyx, from the midst of which springs an upright petal. Usually the fillet is absent, and the stalk is not triparted, but merely a straight stem.

TYPES OF FLEURS-DE-LIS.

Examples of this are seen in the flowers among Egyptian hieroglyphics in the Louvre, and Assyrian sculptures in the British Museum. The type is comparatively rare in heraldry. Dr. Bonavia regards this as the only true representative of *Lilium candidum,* or Madonna lily.

ROYAL ARMS OF ENGLAND (JAMES I).

FLEURS DE LIS AND DOLPHINS.

The outer leaves in the best examples are not too large, and are well curved over. If of nearly the same size as the central petal, and made to stand upright with only their tips curved, an awkward combination is the result. Frequently the under curved edge is serrated, unlike any true lily leaf.

The central petal may be long with a slight globular swelling near the top, or it may be of a more nearly oval form. Other favourite shapes are the squat club-like leaf seen on the Denderah sceptre, and the long diamond, of which rather handsome specimens are seen on French illuminations and on carved work taken to Scotland by Queen Mary Stuart. As a rule the petal is unmarked, but occasionally it has a ridge down the centre, giving it a convex appearance. This is particularly noticeable in the pike or lance-head designs, in which the central lobe is made to assume the appearance of a double-edged weapon with more or less curved cutting edges. However, it also characterises the three herbaceous-leaved lis, such as that seen as early as 1199 on the civic seal of Lille.

Perhaps the most puzzling part of the emblem is the fillet. It has no counterpart in the lily or iris, unless we take it to be a somewhat clumsy rendering of the calyx base, which has a rather marked series of protuberances in some of these flowers. This base may also account for the stalk of our typical lis. The fillet may be a thin, small band, constricting the emblem, or holding the separate parts together. At other times it is thick and long, very prominent. It is sometimes treated like a coronet fillet and studded with jewels. It may be double or even triple. Dr. Bonavia regards this as the essential part of the fleur-de-lis, which betrays its symbolical value. To him the fillet is a ligature, attaching two curved horns to an upright tree symbol. He argues that the central lobe is the Assyrian date palm, and the curved outer petals and their stalks are the luck bringing, evil spirit banishing sacred horns, actually attached to the trees. This theory is, of course, equally applicable to those lis which are shown with the outer curved parts springing from the fillet itself, and having only a central stalk. In the first case he sees two pairs of horns, in the second only one pair. This would be giving a definite birthplace to the symbol, which may have been brought to Europe either by the Crusading knights, or much earlier by means of the far-reaching Phœnician commerce.

As regards the heraldic stalk, we may have three short stems ; a short central and two long outwardly curved stalks ; a central long spike and two short curves ; or we may have practically a replica of the top part, and this repetition may be given such prominence as to detract from the elegance of the design. So far is this carried, indeed, that a double fleur-de-lis may be produced, as in the example drawn by Rey from a shield on a church at Altramura in the province of Naples. It appears to be the result of design, and not a mere whimsical exaggeration. It is constructed much on the principle of Jupiter's thunderbolt. Curiously enough we find a very similar object on the reverse of a British coin, ascribed to a king of the Iceni about A.D. 50. In many cases—and this is a characteristic of most of the badge lis on our Great Seals —the three petals and fillet form a single part, while the stalk is a small three-branched attachment.

It must be confessed that many European artists, even in early times, treated the symbol as though composed of three distinct parts, bound together by the fillet. Thus we have a central globular or lanceolate blossom with two leaves, each with distinct stalk, and not touching each other. In two quaint examples found on seals affixed to abbey charters in France this independence of parts is made quite plain.

GUILLAUME
BARON, 1260.

That on the seal of Theobald de Blangy, recorded at Bayeux, consisted of an upright ear of wheat between two ragged leaves. That of Robert Mahias, Knight Templar (Abbaye d'Aunay), has a central twig with alternate lanceolate leaves (perhaps this, too, may be an ear of wheat), between leaves having an upright shoot and an outward curved part. In this latter example there is no ligament. Yet in both instances, which belong to the thirteenth century, the general outline

of the lis is preserved.   Other examples closely allied to these
are recorded at Aunay, Caen, and so on.   This idea of the
fruitfulness of the symbol is shown in another way.   Often
(both in heraldic painting and sculpture)
the central lobe (and sometimes the three)
is treated as though it were a pod partly
burst and showing seed within.   Or again
we may have birds connected with the
emblem.   On the seal of Guillaume Baron,
Knight Templar (Abbaye d'Aunay, 1260),
we have a lis treated rather architecturally,
the central lobe being a long oval cartouche
with a fillet, apparently to represent a bud,
between two curved leaves with serrated

NORMAN FLEUR-
DE-LIS, 13TH
CENTURY.

under parts, and a fillet.   Standing on each leaf is a small bird
pecking at the central bud.   On the seal of Raoul de Carpiquet
(Abbaye de la Sainte Trinité, Caen) is a fleur-de-lis composed of a curving calyx, fillet and triparted plain stalk,
and a central oval seed pod, whence springs a sprig
with seven filaments, having trefoil buds at the ends.   Clinging to the pod on each side is a bird pecking at the lowest
blossom.   On the ancient seal of the town of Liskeard, Cornwall, we find a large fleur-de-lis, with filaments between the
centre and outer petals, and on the anthers of these filaments
are perched two small birds.   I at first thought that these
small birds were originally intended for the eagles of Richard,
second son of King John, King of the Romans and Earl of
Cornwall, for both he and his son Edmond used a sable
eagle of Rome and the bezants of Cornwall ; while another
Earl of Cornwall, Piers de Gaveston, bore : vert, six eagles
displayed or.   But it was pointed out to me that the parish
church of Liskeard was dedicated to St. Martin of Tours.
Therefore they are probably allusive symbols, two martins.
No doubt this explains the presence of the birds on the Liskeard seal, but those on the seals of the Crusading French
knights suggest a curious connection with birds, winged figures,
and men shown in Eastern symbolism as always guarding
sacred trees, which Sir George Birdwood regarded as the

" witnesses " in connection with phallic worship. Did the supporting angels of the French king's golden lilies come from the same region ?

May we explain that extraordinary anomaly, the leopard's head, *jessant de lis*, in which we see a lis thrust through the mouth of a leopard, the stalk between its teeth and the three petals coming out at the back of its head, by a metamorphosis of the Egyptian and Hindu god-bearing lotus ? On a beautiful sardonyx intaglio in the Demidoff Collection (shown in C. W. King's " Antique Gems and Rings ") we see Cupid rising from a pomegranate flower. On a sceptre shown in a painting at the Bibliothèque Nationale, Paris, attributed to a Roman consul A.D. 525, we see a winged child issuing from a lis. A gold sceptre found in the tomb of Philippe le Bel, at St. Denis, had a serrated leaf on each side of a rod topped by an eagle with half-spread wings. All these look very much like steps in the degeneration of the seed-bearing flower symbol.

The filament almost invariably springs upwards between the three petals, although a few rare instances are found of

FLORENTINE
FLEUR-DE-LIS.

fleurs-de-lis with filaments springing from the ligature outside the curved petals. Generally the filament bears at its end some kind of anther. This may be a mere ball, a concretion of small balls, or, as in the case of the so-called St. Louis example, it may take the form of a well-marked trefoil. On some early Florentine coins the anther partakes of the character of a trident, or an open fleur-de-lis. A daisy ornament tip is also met with as well as starred blossoms. When there is the filament with anther, and the petals are more or less decorated with serrations, curved over leaves, perhaps enclosing seeds, English heralds call it a " fleur-de-lis flowery." The French speak of it as *épanoui*, and the Italians as *giglio Fiorentino*.

A quaint form of decoration adopted by a few early herald painters was to diaper the three petals ; that is, to cover them with running floral or simple geometric patterns drawn in very faint lines. Occasionally examples of diapered fleurs-de-lis are met with in carvings and on seals.

I have said that the lis belongs to the triparted class of symbols. This is true as a rule, for the pictorial idea appears to guide even the sculptor. But there are exceptions. The Bourbon crest, worn on the helmet and apparently on some of their crowns and coronets, had four curved petals and a central upright bud, either ovular or carved so as to present four club or pike faces. This method has also been adopted with some sceptres, and more commonly when forming architectural finials.

It is generally assumed that the earlier French monarchs bore a lis " without number," " powdered," or " semeé," and that the use of only three, two below and one above, came in with Charles V, some say, as already observed, in honour of the Trinity, others to denote the three races of kings. As a matter of fact, from the earliest times heralds treated the lis as a symbol of such importance that it could be shown singly. The royal shields appear semée, with ten (placed 4, 3, 2 and 1), and with only three, long before Charles's day. It even occurs that the three flowers may be borne not as a pyramid, but placed two above and one below, technically, " mal ordonée." While most herald painters did not hesitate to slice off the lis in any way when decorating a " powdered " field, others strove to get in regular lines and only show complete flowers. But in course of time there was evolved a variety named a " fleur-de-lis au pied nourri," when only the top petals and filaments are shown. It was evidently derived from the royal sceptre or crown, and was probably an augmentation granted by kings as a mark of honour.

In England the fleur-de-lis was used at least as early as the first half of the eleventh century. A good specimen is seen on the coins of Harthacnut (1039–41). It is also seen on the coins of Edward the Confessor and of Harold. On the Great Seal of Edward we find the king holding a sceptre with a trefoil, three well-marked lobes forming a cross. On his crown we see trefoils round the band, but in the centre there appears to be a distinct fleur-de-lis. On the Conquerer's coins we find a lis sceptre and a flory cross. Henry II has a crown decorated with lis on his Great Seal, and so had the Empress Matilda, but her sceptre is tipped with a trefoil, not cruciform like the Confessor's, but approaching the form of the lis. After this the symbol appears on the whole series of our Great Seals. The sword of Edward I has a pommel shaped like a lis. On Edward III's first Great Seal we see a large castle on both sides of his throne, and above these a small top-heavy lis, the three petals being of almost equal size, and the stalk very small. On his second seal the castles disappear and we have two large lis, with a big lanceolate upright petal and two well-curved leaves, below the fillet small but well-defined stalks. On his third Great Seal we find the monarch on horseback,

TYPES OF FLEURS-DE-LIS.

with a shield quarterly, France ancient and England. These arms are on the horse's neck and hind quarters, while the background is diapered with lozenges containing a lis. The reduction of the fleur-de-lis to three on the royal coat-of-arms first appears on the second Great Seal of Henry IV. Henry VI had a special seal for French affairs. Thereon we see him with a fleur-de-lis sceptre : on his right is a crowned shield bearing the three lilies, on his left a shield quarterly France and England. On the coins of Henry VII we find both the fleur-de-lis and also a fleur-de-lis dimidiated with a rose. Elizabeth has on her second seal two big épanoui examples, with very small filaments, and each petal shaped as a separate bud enclosing seeds. With the House of Hanover the lis often becomes deplorably squat, sometimes looking much like ill-drawn three ostrich feathers.

St. Louis of France used many forms of the fleur-de-lis. On one of his seals it appears as a compact flower, with lanceolate central petal and two filaments with trefoil tips. It is sometimes named after him, but this variety was used both before and after his time. Indeed, many of St. Louis's lis are very suggestive of metal work—lance heads, pierced and otherwise.

Artists have often adorned the petals, sometimes placing a small crown on the centre lobe, or topping it with a Latin or a Lorraine cross. We have already seen that the side leaves may bear birds. But in heraldry the lis is never charged with another object ; on the other hand it is sometimes placed on a rose, castle, etc., and it may be dimidiated : for instance, half a rose and half a lis being stuck together, or half a lis and half an eagle. Its decorative value is very great.

Apart from its splendid possibilities for shield adornment, the fleur-de-lis became extraordinarily prolific in heraldry as a result of the liberality with which it was granted by both the French and the English kings as a mark of favour to armigerous persons. The change of the Chateaubriand golden pine cones for fleurs-de-lis, as already described, is an example of this. Charles VII bestowed on the brothers of Jeanne d'Arc the name of Lys, together with the following coat-of-arms : azure, a sword in pale argent, pommelled gold, supporting a royal crown on its point, between two fleurs-de-lis, also gold. Louis XII gave to Piero de Medici a roundel azure, thereon three fleurs-de-lis, to add to his collection of five bezants on his shield, for his military and political assistance. Other instances of the bestowal of lis have already been cited. Among these was the adornment of the Scottish tressure border with fleurs-de-lis. Crosses and other ordinaries and charges so decorated probably had a similar origin. Two of the oddest of these additions are seen on the shields of Woodmartin and Goldington, who bear respectively: (1) per fess dancetté argent and sable, each point ending in a fleur-de-lis; (2) or, a bend fleury counter-fleury, azure.

FLEURS-DE-LIS ÉPANOUI.

This last was much like the "bende d'aszure fleureté d'or" borne by Sir Motas de Latimer in the days of Edward II. Among the early English coats worthy of note are the following three. Robert Agulon (*temp.* Henry III) bore: gules, a fleur-de-lis argent. Sir John Deyville (*temp.* Edward II) bore: or, on a fess gules three fleurs-de-lis gold, between three fleurs-de-lis gules. But his descendant, Robert Deyville (*temp.* Edward III), bore: or, on a fess gules four fleurs-de-lis; whether gold or silver is not stated.

This emblem was also widely distributed among towns admitted to royal patronage. A notable example of this is, of course, the city of Paris. As now borne the arms are: gules, an antique ship with sail set, swimming on the river in base; on a chief azure, semée of fleurs-de-lis. But on the seal of the city of 1358 only two fleurs-de-lis appear, one on

ROYAL ARMS OF ENGLAND (JAMES I).

each side of the sail. In the seal of 1366, these have disappeared, but the ship flies a flag bearing three full and part of a fourth fleur-de-lis. Then the lis appear in the sky at the back of the ship, and it is only from 1426 onwards that the blue chief charged with fleurs-de-lis appears.

As already stated, true lilies have been otherwise distinctly conventionalised for ages past. On the Jewish shekels the lilies are the lilies of the field, shown on a rod with blossoms bell-shaped with trilobe petals. The Madonna lilies, as introduced in Christian art, and thence finding their way into heraldry, are quite clearly of the garden type, as may be seen on monastic and other seals. An excellent example is afforded by the arms of Eton College, for on their coat we have both the religious lilies and the royal fleur-de-lis. The arms granted by Henry VI to the College of St. Mary at Eton are : sable, three lilies slipped argent, on a chief per pale azure and gule a fleur-de-lis or, and a lion passant guardant or (of England). These same lilies appear on the coat of Magdalen College, Oxford : fusilly ermine and sable, on a chief of the last three lilies slipped in fess argent. These are the arms of the founder, William Waynflete, Bishop of Winchester, whose real name was Patyn. He added the chief to his paternal coat in acknowledgment of his debt to Eton College. Waynflete appears to have given the chief to Winchester College as well. Then we have the three silver lilies, in association with the golden roses of the Abbey of Barking, these flowers symbolising the Saviour and the Virgin.

As having much direct influence on the growth of the emblems, something must be said here concerning the lotus. This is a water-lily whose blossoms, buds and leaves enter largely into the whole range of decorative and symbolic art of Egypt and the East. The motifs were adopted by the Greeks and spread over Southern and Western Europe through Roman influence. It is a symbol of life and fertility. In Egypt the flower is white with a pink base ; in Persia it is blue ; in India red. The flower is represented in cup form, with large, broad petals, terminating in points, and has a golden seeded centre. The leaves are large and heart-shaped.

Both leaves and blossoms are borne on long, sinuous stems, and in Egyptian art are often found in combination with the papyrus plant, which has a bell-shaped flower and rush-like leaves. The Egyptians drew the blossoms as open in plan, as cup-like flowers in profile and as squat cone-shaped buds. The buds are often conventionalised, and we see a central club-like bud between two petals turned over to right and left, a primitive form of the fleur-de-lis ; it is frequently seen ornamenting the tips of sceptres. The buds, leaves and sinuous stalks are also employed to decorate friezes. A favourite combination of the lotus and papyrus is seen in the Egyptian column, which is either fluted or painted to represent a bundle of leaves, while the capital is in the form of a papyrus bell flower growing out of a lotus. The Persian blue and the Indian red lotus are generally represented as open blossoms, with two rows of pointed petals and a golden seed centre, and are allied in character and symbolism with the chrysanthemum of Japan. Vishnu is often represented as springing from a lotus, as is the youthful Horus, under the form of Harpocrates, the Egyptian god of love.

CHAPTER XVI

THE ROSE

QUEEN of Flora's glowing treasures the rose has long held a proud place in symbolism and in pure decorative art. It is the flower of innocence and of knowledge, of peace and of suffering, of passion and of secrecy. It was the flower sacred to worshippers of Adonis as a token of love and sacrifice, of life springing afresh from dead things. Legend says that Aphrodite hastening to the aid of Adonis, wounded unto death by the Boar of Mount Lebanon, trod on a white rose, thus staining the immaculate flower with immortal ichtor. According to Indian tradition in the Garden Paradise of the Brahmans is a great white rose, wherein are seen two lovely women, the Lady of the Mouth and the Lady of the Tongue, who, however, are one, and in the centre of the Silver Rose the Supreme Being has His permanent abode. Buddha was crucified for despoiling the sacred garden of a white rose, which thereupon became red. Again, it was amidst the frolics of Dionysius, or Bacchus, Cupid and Ganymede that the ruby nectar was spilled, causing the pallid blossoms to blush. These two seemingly divergent ideas (but really coming from the same root notion of the alliance between pleasure and sorrow, joy and sacrifice) rule the whole complicated symbolism of roses in the domain of decoration. So we find the flowers associated by the ancients with festivity, the roses with which they made chaplets to crown their heads as they quaffed libations to Bacchus and the mother of Cupid, which thus suggested the sacredness of words spoken at ceremonial mysteries or in friendly confidence. Adopted as a Christian emblem of He Who represents the Supreme Sacrifice, by a natural transmission, it was attributed to the Virgin Mary, whence we have rosaries, the beads corresponding to petals.

It is this flower that we find so lavishly displayed, occultly or otherwise, down the ages from a far-off past. In its earliest form both archæologically and in primitive heraldry, it is a conventionalised form of the wild or briar rose that we see. The rosettes seen on Phœnician sepulchral stelæ in the British Museum, and carved on soap-stone cylinders in those puzzling South African ruins at Zimbabwe, are practically identical with the quatrefoils and cinquefoils of heraldry, which are really the roses of feudal blazonry. These "daisy-like flowers" found on private and regal seals are the blossoms of the briar, emblematically and glyptically so apt to verge into the radiant star. Strictly speaking the quatrefoils and cinquefoils are formed respectively of four or five oval or squat club-like petals joined together. The quatrefoils are usually pierced of the field, having a circular hole in the centre. With the quatrefoil there is often a cruciform slit, with a pierced or raised centre. Sometimes the petals are slightly concave or convex, but quite as frequently perfectly flat. They may be of any tincture. Vincent bore : azure, three quatrefoils argent. The town of Leicester, for instance, bears : gules, a cinquefoil, pierced of the field, ermine. These are the arms of the powerful family of Beaumont, Earls of Leicester, whose bearings were borne by many other houses in blood or feudal alliance with the great earls. In the reign of Edward I the Lords Astley bore : azure, a cinquefoil ermine ; and under that monarch, at the siege of Carlaverock Hugh Bardoulf emblazoned his banner and shield azure, three cinquefoils or. Gilbert de Umfreville, Earl of Angus (1290), bore : gules, crusily, a cinquefoil or.

Apart from these somewhat nondescript charges, the rose has been treated in heraldry both conventionally and realistically, with equally charming effect. Certainly the early heraldic rose is modelled on the wild type. It is of this variety that Vulson de la Colombière says : " It forms a perfect symbol of beauty and gracefulness, although it

A BRANCH OF THREE ROSES, WITH ROSE SCREEN.

possesses thorns and is doomed to fade." "The rose and the lily," declares the worthy squire, "are united in close amity, for the blending of these two flowers compose and truly represent the colour peculiar to the most perfect of human loveliness," so evidently he was thinking of the red rose, which is by far the most frequently seen in old blazonings. De Brue, a Crusader from Brittany (*circa* 1191), bore: argent, a rose of six petals gules, seeded or. In a Roll of Arms of the reign of Henry III we find Philip Darcy bearing: argent, three roses gules. In another Roll, of Edward II, Sir Robert Darcy is shown bearing: argent, three roses gules, within a border indented sable. His kinsman, Sir John Darcy, had: sable, a border argent charged with red roses. But at the siege of Carlaverock Simon de Fresel (or Fraser) bore: sable, six roses argent; and a later Darcy of Platten bore: azure, three roses between seven crosses bottony argent. With regard to Fraser, it is to be noted that later his roses were converted into "fraisiers," and heraldically there is practically no difference between a strawberry flower and a cinquefoil.

This heraldic rose consists of petals, usually five in the early type; small green leaves (the "barbs") between each pair of petals, representing the sepals of the calyx; and stamens, or cluster of "seeds." It is rarely "leaved and slipped" or "stalked." The petals are generally heart-shaped, slightly cup-like, with upward curving edges. Sometimes the barbs show between the petals, but more often only the tips appear at the edges. The "seeds" may be treated as a collection of tiny round balls, or the circular space is criss-crossed like a tartlet. In later examples two or more rows of petals are used, when we have a conventionalised rendering of the garden flower, as in the Tudor rose. Of course, this is merely a development and embellishment of the ancient rosette.

Side by side with this, however, a more realistic flower was being used. We hear of Edward I having for badge a gold rose with green stalk and leaves. In the oft-quoted Roll of Arms of Henry III, we are told that Le Comte de Rampanile bore: "dor a treis rosers; sur chekune roser une rose; chekune roser verte." These probably were rose branches, or slips, though they may have been rose bushes. Apparently, the field being gold, it was thought unnecessary to specify that the roses were red.

As for Edward's golden rose, it may have been derived from his mother, or perhaps borne in memory of her. For she was Eleanor, daughter of Raymond of Provence, where a cultivated variety of this flower had been introduced by Thibault IV and his knights on their return home from Cru-

TUDOR ROSE EN SOLEIL WITH THE ARROW BADGE OF ARAGON.

sading. Roses of Provence were celebrated, and quickly found their way into local heraldry. A good example is afforded by the coat of d'Espinassy, of that province : or, a rose between three buds proper, slipped and leaved sable. These dusky blooms were of the botanical type. Edward III decorated his Great Seal with small roses, and his grandson, Richard II, placed them on Garters which he bestowed on a few honoured courtiers. But it was most likely from the exotic rose, rather than from the " daisy-like flower " and the briar blooms on the Great Seals, that the famous Yorkist and Lancastrian badges were derived. It is surmised that John of Gaunt, Duke of Lancaster, fourth son of Edward III, adopted the red rose, for cadets often used their fathers' cognisances somewhat differenced. In spite of the generally received idea, there is no direct evidence that the white rose belonged to Edmond of Langley, Duke of York, fifth son of Edward III. It seems far more likely that it was assumed by Edmond's second son, Richard of Coningsburgh, Duke of Cambridge, for he took as his second wife Maud, daughter of Thomas, Lord Clifford. From a manuscript in the Harleian Collection we see that a white rose was the badge of the Castle of Clifford, possibly in allusion to " Fair Rosamond " of Clifford. However this may be, these two badges were worn on a lavish scale during the long-drawn-out dynastic turmoil known in history as the Wars of the Roses. Edward IV, who had a diaper of small cinquefoil-roses and stars on his Great Seal (a design copied by Richard III on his Great Seal), placed his white rose on the Sun in Splendour badge of Richard II. Thus was produced the first of a long line of " roses en soleil," for both the red rose and the united blooms were later treated in the same manner.

To what extent the " wearing of the rose " entered into the national life may be gathered even by considering the byways of land tenure. A few out of many instances are worthy of mention. Sir Marmaduke Darel held the Manor of Fulmer, Bucks, direct from the King by the service of one red rose yearly (*temp*. Henry VI), while the Buckinghamshire Darrells bore : azure, a lion rampant or ; a branch of that family had : argent, three bars sable, on the first bar three silver roses. Sandes held land at Northampton from the King at a rental of one rose. In 1348 Sir John Poulteney " gave and confirmed to Humfrey de Bohun, Earl of Hereford and Essex, his whole tenement called Cold Harborough [Coal Harbour] with all the tenements and key adjoining, and appurtenances, on the way called Hay Wharf-lane for one rose at midsummer." Some overlords, however, actually stipulated for a rose at Christmas and a snowball at Midsummer, which was tantamount to a tenancy terminable at will of the grantor. We find that Edward Leigh in the thirty-second year of the reign of Queen Elizabeth died possessed of the Rose Hospital in West Smithfield, but this was almost certainly in allusion to the religious emblem. That was evidently the case as regards the Rose Manor in Southwark, which was referred to as a messuage called the Rose when Edward VI made over the Manor of Southwark to the City of London. We know that Henslowe and Alleyne's Rose Theatre must have been close by. Edward Alleyne received a grant of arms, which were: argent, a chevron between three cinquefoils gules. Now, he left his fortune for educational purposes and to benefit his native parish of St. Botolph, Bishopsgate, and the parishes of St. Olave's and St. Saviour's, where he had amassed much of his wealth. It is interesting to find the tradition still carried on, for St. Olave's and St. Saviour's Grammar School as late as 1668 gave a lease of a certain field (which has become very valuable property) for over five hundred years, at a rental of a red rose annually.

However, to return to the royal badge of the radiant rose. Sometimes the rays, which are almost always of gold, project equally on all sides, producing a series of circles; but as a rule they are of varying lengths, arranged in such a way as to give the composition a diamond shape. This figure is seen placed within a mascle (or pierced diamond), and that again within a voided (or outlined) quatrefoil, the words "Dieu et mon droit" being written in the open spaces of the lobes. Henry VII, having united the opposing factions by his marriage with his cousin, blended the two badges, producing the Tudor rose. The first of these was borne quarterly red and white.

ROSE EN SOLEIL BADGE.

More generally the Tudor rose consisted of a row of red petals, then a row of white, and the golden circle in the middle, the bloom having three or more rows of petals round the golden "seeds." Occasionally the roses were dimidiated, being united per fess or per pale, one half red and the other half white. There are often more than two rows,

BADGE OF RICHARD, DUKE OF YORK AND EARL OF CAMBRIDGE.

when the colours alternate row by row, not petal by petal. These Tudor types are usually barbed, rarely stalked and leaved, though instances occur of this, and also their appearance on slips and bushes. Thus in a manuscript of the Heralds' College we find that Henry bore "a red rose surmounted of a white rose, with two buds slipped vert." They are treated as "roses en soleil," and Sandford gives a curious

specimen in his genealogical work on our Royal Houses, for
it bears in the centre a small crucifix.   Martin Luther appears
to have used as badge a red heart ensigned with a black cross,

placed in the middle of a silver
rose, surrounded by the golden
circle of Eternity, the whole on
a blue field.   These may be
compared to the Buddhist
legend already given, and to
the mystic symbol of the
Rosicrucians, a white or silver
rose on a red cross—the crucified rose.   Henry VII placed
on his Great Seal a Tudor rose
on each side of the throne ;
the background of the obverse
is fretty and powdered with
roses and fleurs-de-lis, the latter
being fixed at the intersections

MARTIN LUTHER'S BADGE.

of the frets and the roses in the interspaces.   On his standard
he bore both the red and white roses, barbed and seeded proper,
separately.   Henry VIII, who had on the obverse side of
his Great Seal a large Tudor rose in the sky, and two more
on the caparisons of his charger, bore the stalked white rose
within a red rose with two buds, like his father, as well as a
separate red rose.

With his wives and children, even greater variety was introduced.   Catherine of Aragon united her native pomegranate
with the roses of her adopted country.   In the early examples
this was done in a strange way, the seed pod is shown bursting
on both sides, the dexter exposing the purple pomegranate
grains, the sinister showing a half-emerging Tudor rose.
Later, thorough dimidiation per pale was adopted, and this
badge Henry bore at a tournament in honour of his queen.
Round her coat-of-arms she placed a wreath of livery colours,
the white and green ribbons entwining red and white roses
and golden pomegranates.   Anne Boleyn's chief badge was
a golden stump of a tree, with a crowned falcon standing

thereon, bearing a sceptre in his sinister claw, while in front of it were rows of red and white roses on green stalks. Jane Seymour had a curious circular double silver castle; over

TUDOR ROSE, QUARTERLY RED
AND WHITE.

ROSE AND POMEGRANATE, BADGE
OF CATHERINE OF ARAGON.

the port was a hawthorn bush proper, flowered gules, and crowned; while on the green mound of the upper tower a golden crowned phœnix rose from flames of fire, a red and a white rose stalked vert being on either side of the pyre. Catherine Parr united the Tudor rose with her own family badge, derived from Ross of Kendal, of a demi-crowned queen. The arrangement is rather odd than pretty. Above small green barbs we see a row of four large red petals, then three of white, with a row of four smaller leaves of red, and out of the top of this pyramid issues a demi-queen proper, crowned,

BADGE OF CATHERINE PARR.

habited and crinned gold. Edward VI had much the same design for his Great Seal as that of his father, only the Tudor roses in his case are crowned, and on the obverse, in the foreground is a stump of a tree sending forth a network of fine argent between three rose leaves silver, we have petals. A curious bearing is that of Tudman : argent, two bars azure, over all a lion rampant or, holding in the dexter paw a rose branch gules, probably referring to some family alliance. But we also see a wild boar with a rose and leaves in its mouth. Alten bears : argent, a bend of lozenges and roses alternately disposed gules.

CHAPTER XVII

THE IRISH HARP IN HERALDRY

HERALDICALLY the Irish harp is a thing of no great antiquity, owing its birth to the political instability of Henry VIII. As a racial token it becomes a link between the moon-worshippers' cup-markings and the three conjoined legs (naked in sunny Sicily, clothed in Mona), types of the Trinacria of the Latins, the Triskele of Scandinavians, themselves mere forms of the sun-worshippers' cramponed cross-wheel, that elaboration of the curved crossed snakes or swastika of the East. For the Welsh bardic harp and the Irish cruit were alike enlisted in the praise of Baal, the sun god, bestower of life, whose powerful rays gave rise to elemental harmonics. The bard and his instrument were held in high honour by Celt and Cymri, and the Saxon poets called the harp " the wood of joy." It might form an interesting subject of inquiry whether the Tudor prince in adopting a new badge for his kingdom of Ireland had not been guided by Welsh traditions, domestic or political.

Long prior to the rise of the House of Tudor the official arms of Ireland had been three golden crowns in pale on a blue field. These were the mythical arms of Edmund, King and Martyr, and probably owed their transplantation to the fact that the Anglo-Norman invaders, when setting about their conquest, invoked the protection of St. Edward and St. Edmund. These crowns were so far recognised that we find them on the Irish coinage, and when Richard II created Robert Vere Duke of Ireland, he assigned him as an augmentation to his arms, a blue field with three gold crowns, borne two in base and one in chief. Misliking these symbols for

their supposedly Romish symbolism, Bluff King Hal established an undatably ancient Celtic emblem of concord as the
national badge. Its first appearance seems to have been
on his Irish silver sixpenny-piece, struck in the thirty-eighth
year of his reign. It is found on the back, crowned, and
between the small crowned letters H and R. Its form is
decidedly peculiar, for we find its sounding-board broadening
upwards, and its seven pairs of strings stretched between the
neck and front pillar. Thus it is a complete reversal of the

musical   instrument.
Much the same shape was
retained on the Irish
coins of Mary, Philip and
Mary,   and   Elizabeth,
though the harp is longer
and more upright, but
the topsy-turvy idea still
prevails.

A legend, fabricated
long after the event, tells
us that this harp of Henry
VIII was the instrument
which once awoke sweet
echoes within the marble
halls of Tara, seat of the
suzerain kings of Erin.

IRISH HARP, *temp.* HENRY VIII.

This antique relic of Brian
Boru was supposed to have been sent by the Pope to King
Henry VIII, though there is no evidence that it ever was in
Rome, or in London. Some years after that robust swash-
buckler and conqueror Brian was slain at the battle of Clontarf,
A.D. 1014, his son Donogh murdered his brother Teague. As a
reward for his villainy he was deposed ; but he astutely took
possession of his father's crown, harp and regalia (so runs the
legend), with which he fled to Rome to make his peace with
the Pope. Adrian IV, it is said, claimed that holding these
regalia he became manifestly King of Ireland, which war-
ranted the transference of these rights to Henry II. Of this

regalia, as further evidence of royalty, Henry VIII received the harp. So far tradition. It is certain that a very old, richly decorated harp, said to be the identical instrument, is preserved in the Museum of Trinity College, Dublin, but Dr. George Petrie, in a learned article contributed to Edward Bunting's "Ancient Music of Ireland" (1840), proves that the harp really belongs to the fourteenth century, or perhaps even the early part of the fifteenth century. It is a beautiful instrument, 32 inches high, with a sound-board of red sallow, a pillar of oak, and a neck of such charming contour that it has been named the "harmonic curve." The sound-board has four holes and there are thirty strings. The whole harp is richly adorned with carvings of modified Celtic ornamentation, silver, brass and crystal incrustations, and bears a rude representation of the O'Neil arms, as well as religious initials. From its form and decoration Dr. Petrie held that it probably belonged to one of those O'Neils who flourished as Bishops of Clogher and of Derry during the latter end of the fourteenth century. In this connection it is perhaps interesting to note that the Bishops of Derry now bear a harp on their coat-of-arms.

Although this instrument had nothing to do with Henry VIII, it is interesting because undoubtedly very old ; thus demonstrating the true form of the Irish harp. It is the form which should prevail on our royal and national escutcheon. The true guiding lines for the Irish heraldic harp are those of the scalene triangle: the long straight line (sound-board) leaning slightly back, the shorter line (pillar) bulging outwards, and the top line (neck), curving inwards. These lines —as we shall see—were abandoned, the isosceles triangle becoming the base of the draughtsman's sketch ; then by an easy transition (*facilis descensus averni*), the neck was stretched out and we had the almost perfect equilateral triangle, which practically prevailed up to within the last twenty years. The error is an unfortunate one, though it must be confessed not the worst treatment meted out to the symbol.

A crowned harp appears on the counter seal of Elizabeth's

13

second Great Seal. It is in the form of a badge. It is of excellent shape, for in conventionalising the emblem the artist retained the true main lines.

When James I ascended the throne, the Irish harp was, for the first time, introduced on the royal shield, the fourth quarter being emblazoned : azure, a harp or, stringed argent. The harps shown in the two Great Seals of James are fairly good, though there is a quaint neck added on the top of the sounding-board to connect it with the true neck, while the front pillar is too straight. The crowned badge harps on the counter seals are purely conventional ; they become spade shaped, the neck showing an inverted semicircle, little difference being made between the sound-board and pillar. We find the spade harps on James's gold sovereigns and double crowns, and his silver sixpences. It is on his coins that the erroneous equilateral triangle begins to prevail. The lines are also too florid ; the sound-board is made quite short, a slim curved arm, to connect it with the neck, being added. Moreover, the end of the neck is brought too far over, and, being unduly ornamented, foreshadows that other grievous sin, the feminine headed harp. At first, the end is merely a floral embellishment, but in his later gold coins and in the money struck in Ireland, it becomes distinctly the head of an animal. In the Irish form it is the head of some fabulous bird. I conjecture this was an Anglo-Saxon enormity, for in an illuminated coat-of-arms of James I by Sir William Segar, Garter King (Harleian MSS.), the pillar and forearm of the harp are joined by the mask of a satyr, a wild man of the woods, for the features are devoid of the culture and repose we should associate with the inspired bard.

With Charles I the equilateral triangle outline is pronounced. On the early coins and Great Seals the ornamentation is too florid, though the Celtic idea is not lost sight of. The flourish at the neck end, however, soon develops into a beak. In another illuminated MS. (Harleian Collection), we find the mask of a leopard. But the form of this harp is altogether rustically eccentric. It is to be noted that we find two tendencies at work here, the desire to join the neck and pillar by a knob, or mask, and, on the other hand, the development of the florid curved ends into heads, hair and wings. The head is first finished off with floral continuations, then it gradually develops a well-marked bust, terminating in foliated drapery, as we have it to the end of the Victorian period, and the simple bowed pillar is gone. From the head sprout floral adjuncts, which eventually become wings, and so the gracefully curved neck of the instrument is lost. The full-fledged female harp is also an English invention. It makes its first appearance on the silver crown-piece struck at York, which consequently cannot be earlier than 1629. We also find it on the two St. Patrick's halfpennies, so-called because they bear on the reverse effigies of St. Patrick exhibiting a shamrock to assembled disciples in one instance, and banishing reptiles in a second.

IRISH HARP, *temp.* JAMES I.

The obverse of both of these coins bears a crown, and the kneeling figure of David crowned playing the harp. These harps, though differing slightly, have the winged female figure, with bust well developed.

It is to be presumed that the heralds, having evolved a female form out of the chaos of their florid scrolls, dubbed her Erin. There seems evident intention of symbolism in the later forms of the figure.

Some time towards the latter end of the seventeenth century the French heralds tried their hands at the Celtic harp, requiring it to emblazon on the regimental flags of the Irish legions in the French king's pay. They produced a weird arrangement, suggestive of an ill-treated gridiron, with a satyr head stuck on one corner.

During the Commonwealth the ugly female harp was frankly adopted. We find it on the first two " geographical " seals, which show excellent maps of England, Wales, and Ireland (Scotland being totally omitted). In the top part of these seals, between England and Ireland, is a shield bearing the arms of St. George, while the harp is seen on a shield just outside the Irish Channel. But apart from the female figure the shape is elegant, scalene triangle lines being perfect, were it not for the woman's obtruding head. The same style of harp, though somewhat more approaching the equilateral triangle, is seen on the Protectorate seals of Oliver and Richard Cromwell. Generally speaking, on the Commonwealth coins the same type of harp is used as that found on the early seals, but there are some variations. The copper farthings have three remarkable patterns, all bad, because deviating from the true lines, while one is absurdly conventional. One of the sixpenny-pieces shows a harp with a very small sound-board, from which a female figure springs, turning her back to the pillar figure, the wings conjoined. On one of the shillings, and on half-crowns, we have a return to the goose and reptile heads.

On the Great Seal of Charles II the Irish harp occupies the second quarter of the shield, and is of a rather novel shape. The sound-board is narrow, upright and short ; the wings forming the neck curving upwards to the head, while the bust and foliated drapery (the pillar) form the segment of a circle. On his coins the harp is of inelegant, squat type, occasionally almost approaching a square, in such instances the head often sticking upright like a useless handle.

With James, Queen Anne, and the sovereigns of the Houses of Orange and of Hanover, little that is new is to be remarked. We can only note a tendency to confirm the equilateral triangle, to develop the female figure, and with the Victorian seals and coins unnecessarily to broaden the sounding-board. On the first Great Seal of George IV, however, on the counter seal, there is an allegorical figure representing Ireland, leaning on a tall harp on the true scalene triangle lines, but remarkable because the pillar is a complete winged female figure, nearly nude.

Meanwhile, a pretty and fairly accurate form of the Irish harp had been evolved from the royal emblems. We find Celtic form usually adhered to in the achievement of Ulster

King of Arms, and also in the modern bearings of the see of Derry.

When Edward VII ascended the throne and became Sovereign of the Ancient and Noble Order of the Garter, it was necessary to have the King's Royal Banner as Chief of the Order in St. George's Chapel, Windsor Castle. This banner was embroidered at the Royal School of Needlework, from the design of Mr. G. W. Eve. He adopted a thoroughly Celtic outline, though perhaps the pillar broadens too much towards the neck. But it was a vast improvement on the female harp. At the last moment objection was raised to this design and the beautiful harp was ruthlessly cut away and replaced by a Victorian instrument. As regards Mr. Eve's design, adverse criticisms were advanced by ultra-scientific heraldists, at the decoration of the harp with Celtic markings, the argument being that a charge should be plain. But in this instance the gold embroidered designs gave a characteristic touch to the Irish harp, and we may well ask why diapering— or the filling up of blank spaces with diminutive conventional designs—should be allowed on a field, and not on a charge, where they happen to emphasise symbolical value. Certainly old herald artists did not hesitate to diaper charges. We should endeavour to retain the Celtic feeling, and the harmonic curve of good Bishop O'Neil's hymnal harp.

IRISH HARP DESIGNED FOR GARTER BANNER OF EDWARD VII.

One or two instances of the harp on the shields of private persons may be given. It appears quite appropriate that Everest should bear: argent a harp gules; Harpfield: argent, three harps sable, stringed or; and Harpman: sable, a harp argent, stringed or. The charge is also found in the arms of Dobbin and Fogarty, and is occasionally met with in Continental practice.

CHAPTER XVIII

FEATHERS AND HORNS

FEATHERS are found under many different aspects. Mention has been made of the polychrome wings of angels, and a good deal will be said about wing and plume crests. Wings when borne in pairs, joined at the pinions, but without a bird's body intervening, are called a " vol " if the points are elevated, or a " vol abased," or " abaisé," if the points are lowered. A single wing is a " demi vol." These wings appeared to be very natural decorations for helmets, and are seen quite early, evidently as survivals of the bird-helmet. But in time they were treated with considerable eccentricity, as we see more particularly on studying German practice in the fourteenth and fifteenth centuries. We find crests of two wings with the lower parts covered with the " eyes " of peacock's feathers, the flight feathers being those of eagles.

In the case of John III, Duke of Brabant, the peacock wing borne has a gold scalloped border, ermine spotted flight feathers, and standing up between the vol is a plume of peacock's feathers. The crest of John, King of Bohemia, appears to have been indifferently a couple of eagle's wings, and a vol, the lower part sprinkled with linden leaves.

Another type consists of the pair of eagle flight feathers borne erect, one on either side of the helmet, as in the case of the Bishop of Cologne, whose plumes are used as flagstaffs. His crest is also interesting as showing another use of feathers, as a decorative border, which is also seen in the case of the Hanoverian crest.

The " panache " might take the form of a compact crown

of several "heights," as in the Mortimer crest, or a plume after the Dacian type. This leads us directly to the famous ostrich plumes of the Princes of Wales. As is well known this crest consists of three grouped silver feathers, the middle one curling forwards, and the others, slightly shorter, curling outwards. Three such feathers were borne by Edward, surnamed the Black Prince, it is said, as a crest or badge. Contemporary evidence, however, shows that he did not bear them as a triparted group, but placed three silver ostrich feathers, each enfiled with a scroll, on a black shield, and this he specifically describes in his will as his "badge of Peace." The best known example of this is from the illuminated charter granting him the Duchy of Aquitaine. It is interesting as showing the realistic treatment of the plumes, and also the purely decorative use of angel supporters. How did the Prince come by this badge? It is matter of doubt and controversy. William Camden gave currency to the legend that the Black Prince took it from the helm of John, King of Bohemia, Duke of Luxem-

CRESTED HELM, JOHN III.
DUKE OF BRABANT.

WINGED HELM, JOHN, KING OF
BOHEMIA.

burg, whom he is supposed to have slain at the battle of Crecy.

SEAL OF COMTE DE PORHOET,
BRITTANY, 1231.

John Aderne, a physician who appears to have been in the service of a knight belonging to the Prince's forces, certainly mentions the story, and in a medical treatise actually gives a picture of the single ostrich feather. But a difficulty arises inasmuch as John of Luxemburg is not known to have used such a crest, for all evidence goes to show that he bore eagle's wings. The only known connection with the family and the plumes is the ostrich badge of Anne of Bohemia, granddaughter of Duke John, and queen of Richard II. But this appears to have been a purely personal badge. Sir Harris Nicolas fancies the plumes really came from Philippa of Hainault, queen of Edward III, and mother of the Black Prince. She is known to have had plate adorned with a black shield with ostrich feathers. Possibly, he conjectured, it may have been a family badge allusive to their County of Ostrevant. There is, however, no evidence of this. But we do know that Edward III on one of his seals placed the

OSTRICH BADGE OF ANNE OF BOHEMIA.

ROSE PATERNOSTER FROM FIFTEENTH-CENTURY BOOK.

BLACK PRINCE'S "SHIELD OF PEACE."